ACADEMIC ENGAGEMENT IN PUBLIC AND POLITICAL DISCOURSE

PROCEEDINGS OF THE MICHIGAN MEETING, MAY 2015

Andrew J. Hoffman, Kirsti Ashworth, Chase Dwelle, Peter Goldberg, Andrew Henderson, Louis Merlin, Yulia Muzyrya, Norma-Jean Simon, Veronica Taylor, Corinne Weisheit, and Sarah Wilson

REPORT OF THE MICHIGAN MEETING ON ACADEMIC ENGAGEMENT

May 13–15, 2015
Rackham Amphitheater
University of Michigan,
Ann Arbor

Steering Committee
Andrew J. Hoffman (chair), Professor and Director, Erb Institute for Global Sustainable Enterprise; Mark Barteau, Professor and Director, Michigan Energy Institute; Gregg Crane, Professor and Director, Program in the Environment; Paul Edwards, Professor of Information; Lianne Lefsrud, Postdoctoral Fellow, Erb Institute for Global Sustainable Enterprise, Dow Sustainability Fellow; Andrew Maynard, Professor and Director, Risk Science Center; Shelie Miller, Associate Professor, School of Natural Resources and Environment; Joy Rohde, Assistant Professor, Gerald R. Ford School of Public Policy; Don Scavia, Professor and Director, Graham Sustainability Institute; David Uhlmann, Professor and Director, Environmental Law and Policy Program

Scribes and Report Writers
Kirsti Ashworth, Research Fellow, Department of Atmospheric, Oceanic and Space Sciences; Chase Dwelle, Dow Doctoral Sustainability Fellow, Department of Civil and Environmental Engineering; Peter Goldberg, Doctoral Student, Department of Chemistry; Andrew Henderson, Doctoral Student, Program in Chemical Biology; Louis Merlin, Dow Postdoctoral Sustainability Fellow, Taubman College of Architecture and Urban Planning; Yulia Muzyrya, Doctoral Student, Ross School of Business; Norma-Jean Simon, Research Associate, Child Health Evaluation and Research Unit; Veronica Taylor, Doctoral Student, Department of Biophysics, Life Sciences Institute; Corinne Weisheit, Doctoral Student, Cellular and Molecular Biology Graduate Program; Sarah Wilson, Dow Doctoral Sustainability Fellow, School of Natural Resources and Environment

Cover illustration by Stephen Leacock—leacockdesign.com

Front inside cover created by Andrew Maynard using weighted keywords selected by the steering committee and scribes to describe the dialogue at the conference.

Conference photographs courtesy of Mark Bialek, Day 1 (http://markbialek.com) and Mike Gould, Days 2 and 3 (http://www.mondodyne.com). Photograph of Jane Lubchenco courtesy of Joy Leighton.

Organizational affiliations are for identification purposes only. The opinions expressed in this report are the sole responsibility of the participants quoted.

This conference is made possible by the sponsorship of the Horace H. Rackham School of Graduate Studies at the University of Michigan. The Michigan Meetings are a series of annual interdisciplinary meetings of national and international scope on topics of broad interest and contemporary importance to both the public and the academic community. Supplemental support for this conference was also provided by the Erb Institute, the Graham Institute, the Michigan Energy Institute, and the Risk Science Center.

Cite as: Hoffman, A., K. Ashworth, C. Dwelle, P. Goldberg, A. Henderson, L. Merlin, Y. Muzyrya, N. Simon, V. Taylor, C. Weisheit, and S. Wilson. *Academic Engagement in Public and Political Discourse: Proceedings of the Michigan Meeting, May 2015*. Ann Arbor, MI: Michigan Publishing, 2015.

Conference web page: http://graham.umich.edu/mm/

© November 2015 Regents of the University of of Michigan, All rights reserved.

Published in the United States of America by Michigan Publishing http://www.publishing.umich.edu/

ISBN 978-1-60785-365-7

Contents

1. Introduction — 1
2. Agenda — 7
3. Summary Report — 11
   - The Presidents' Point of View — 11
     - Why we should engage — 11
     - How to engage — 12
     - Overcoming obstacles to engagement — 14
   - Why Should Academics Engage in Public and Political Discourse? — 15
   - How Should Academics Engage in Public and Political Discourse? — 22
     - Engagement is a two-way dialogue — 22
     - Engagement can yield mutual benefit — 24
     - Know your audience — 24
     - Engagement is political and messy — 28
     - Training, formal and informal — 30
     - Entering the world of politics — 32
   - How Can Institutional Obstacles to Engagement Be Overcome? — 33
   - The Students' Point of View — 36
   - Imagining the Future of Public and Political Engagement — 38

CONTENTS

4. Resources for Academic Engagement in Public and Political Discourse — 41
5. Panel Discussion: Presidents Crow, Hanlon, Sullivan, and Schlissel — 43
6. Delivering on Science's Social Contract — 67
   Jane Lubchenco
7. Summary of Academic Engagement Faculty Survey — 87

Insets:
- Experiences in Engagement: Matthew Davis — 16
- Delivering on Science's Social Contract: Jane Lubchenco — 20
- Good, Bad, and Maybe: Communicating Scientific Near Certainties and Deep Uncertainties to a Nonscientific Audience: Richard Alley — 26
- Experiences in Engagement: Juan Cole — 29
- Experiences in Engagement: Lisa Nakamura — 31

1 INTRODUCTION

This report and the conference it summarizes are an examination of how we as academics practice our craft—how we work to make it more relevant to broader publics and more responsive to pressing societal problems. It is about the kinds of research we conduct, but even more, it is about the public meaning and goals of that work. Ultimately, it is about who we are as a university and what it means to be an academic in a society facing complex scientific, technological, and social challenges. We come to this discussion driven by a deep concern that the academy is facing a crisis of relevance. That crisis is driven by multiple forces that are compelling change.

The first set of forces relates to the quality of the public debate around the critical issues of our day and the limited extent to which academic scholarship informs it. Consider, for example, the current debate over climate change. A recent study found that, of the more than four thousand academic papers that expressed a position on climate change between 1991 and 2011, 97.1 percent agreed that climate change is occurring and is anthropogenic.[1] This is consistent with numerous other studies showing similarly conclusive results[2] and the consensus of more than two hundred scientific agencies around the world.[3] And yet the most recent surveys of public attitudes on climate change show that only 65 percent of American adults believe that there is solid evidence that temperatures on earth have increased during the past four decades,[4] and the number of Americans who believe that "most scientists think global warming is

---

1. Cook, J., D. Nuccitelli, S. Green, M. Richardson, B. Winkler, R. Painting, R. Way, P. Jacobs, and A. Skuce. 2013. "Quantifying the Consensus on Anthropogenic Global Warming in the Scientific Literature." *Environmental Research Letters* 8 (2013). doi: 10.1088/1748-9326/8/2/024024.

2. Oreskes, N. 2004. "The Scientific Consensus on Climate Change." *Science* 306 (5702): 1686.

3. Governor's Office of Planning and Research. 2014. *Scientific Organizations That Hold the Position That Climate Change Has Been Caused by Human Action.* State of California, http://opr.ca.gov/s_listoforganizations.php.

4. Borick, C., and B. Rabe. 2012. *Continued Rebound in American Belief in Climate Change: Spring 2012 NSAPOCC Findings.* Washington, DC: Brookings Institution.

Andrew Hoffman, University of Michigan

happening" declined from 47 percent to 39 percent between 2008 and 2011.[5] More important, there is a sharp partisan divide on this issue with implications for our political discourse at the state and national levels; the latest surveys show that 81 percent of Democrats and 42 percent of Republicans believe there is solid evidence of global warming.[6]

This is but one example of the startling disconnect between the consensus of the academy and the understanding of the general population. A January 2015 Pew Research Center study found a similar divide on other topics: 87 percent of scientists accept that natural selection plays a role in evolution, while only 32 percent of the public agree; 88 percent of scientists think that genetically modified foods are safe to eat, but only 37 percent of the public agree.[7] In a particularly extreme example, many parents have chosen not to vaccinate their children for fear of autism, despite the vehement rejection of that causal link by American medical institutions.

This is a cause for concern. In our increasingly technological world, issues like nanotechnology, stem-cell research, nuclear power, climate change, vaccines and autism, genetically modified organisms, gun control, health care, and endocrine disruption require thoughtful and informed debate. But instead, these and other issues have often been caught up in the so-called culture wars. Though this effect is not uniform—a July 2015 Pew Research Center study found that views on climate change and energy policy are more affected by ideology than those on food safety, space travel, and biomedicine[8]—this problem is exacerbated by the fact that the public is not well versed in science. According to the California Academy of Sciences, the majority of the US public is unable to pass even a basic scientific literacy test.[9] The National Science Foundation reports that two-thirds of Americans do not clearly understand the scientific process.[10] A survey by Research!America found that two-thirds of Americans could not name a single living scientist.

---

5. Ding, D., E. Maibach, X. Zhao, C. Roser-Renouf, and A. Leiserowitz. 2011. "Support for Climate Policy and Societal Action Are Linked to Perceptions about Scientific Agreement." *Nature Climate Change* 1:462–466.
6. Borick and Rabe, 2012.
7. Funk, C., and L. Rainie. 2015, January 29. *Public and Scientists' Views on Science and Policy.* Washington, DC: Pew Research Center.
8. Funk, C., L. Rainie, and D. Page. 2015, July 1. *Americans, Politics and Science Issues.* Washington, DC: Pew Research Center.
9. California Academy of Sciences. 2009. "American Adults Flunk Basic Science." http://www.calacademy.org/newsroom/releases/2009/scientific_literacy.php.
10. National Science Foundation. 2004. "Science and Technology: Public Attitudes and Understanding." *Science and Engineering Indicators 2004,* http://www.nsf.gov/statistics/seind04/c7/c7h.htm.

Of the one-third that could, half named Stephen Hawking.[11] This lack of knowledge coupled with an increased degree of antagonism toward science prompted *National Geographic* in March 2015 to devote its cover story to "The War on Science."

Numerous factors help explain these disconnects between scholars and the public (such as motivated reasoning, political power, and economic interests), but the particular explanation we wish to address in this report is the extent to which the academic and scientific communities have been ineffective or disengaged in explaining the state and gravity of scientific findings. While academics often "believe the public is uninformed about science and therefore prone to errors in judgment and policy preferences," they frequently do not accept any role "as an enabler of direct public participation in decision-making through formats such as deliberative meetings, and do not believe there are personal benefits for investing in these activities."[12] Instead, many remain on the sidelines of important public and political discourse. For the benefit of society's ability to make wise decisions and for the benefit of the academy's ability to remain relevant, the academic community needs to accept some form of public engagement.

There are other forces that extend this crisis of relevance for the academy. First, social media is democratizing knowledge—changing the channels through which science is communicated and who can access them. But the academy is not keeping up. While we write our papers in academic journals and think we have contributed to public discourse, others can publish competing reports and use social media to have far more of an impact on public opinion. Massive open online courses (MOOCs), open-access journals, blogs, and other forms of new educational technology are altering what it means to be a teacher and a scholar. Adding to this changing landscape are a rise in pseudoscientific journals[13] and a growing trend among state legislatures to cut funding to higher education, oftentimes motivated by a professed lack of appreciation for the value that the academy provides to society. These factors, coupled with the rapidly rising cost of higher education, lead to an antagonism toward the academy that has become alarming.

This confluence of forces led *The Economist* to wonder if America's universities could go the way of the Big 3 American car companies, unable to see the cataclysmic changes around them and failing to react. The article cited pressure on faculty to do more research, growing administrative staff, and rising costs. (Median household income has grown by a factor of 6.5 in the past forty years, but the cost of attending state college has increased by a factor of 15 for in-state students and 24 for out-of-state students.)[14]

But all is not lost. Promising changes seem to be afoot. In particular, young people are coming to the academy with a different set of aspirations and goals than their senior advisors. They are speaking with their feet and undertaking outreach and engagement activities on their own. Representative of this growing desire for a more engaged career, of the two hundred academic registrants at this conference, nearly one-third were PhD and postdoctoral students, and they wonder about

---

11. Leif, L. 2015. "Science, Meet Journalism. You Two Should Talk." *The Wilson Quarterly,* January 14.
12. Besley, J., and M. Nisbet. 2013. "How Scientists View the Public, the Media and the Political Process." *Public Understanding of Science,* 22(6): 644–659.
13. Kolata, G. 2013. "Scientific Articles Accepted (Personal Checks Too)." *New York Times,* April 7.
14. Schumpeter columnist. 2010. "Declining by Degree: Will America's Universities Go the Way of Its Car Companies?" *The Economist,* September 2.

the future relevance of the academy and of their careers. They are the future of the academy, and they are changing.

But academic scholars are often not trained or given the proper incentives to engage with the public. Indeed, many of us are culturally biased away from this kind of activity, which is often viewed as a waste of time at best and anti-intellectual at worst. Other academics avoid engagement for fear of being seen as elitist in a contemporary environment that appears to be suspicious of their authority or expertise. Others avoid it because it can be unpleasant. Many scholars who study topical issues like climate change get their regular share of hate mail. And some receive startlingly harsh treatment (from both outside and inside the academy), diminished stature, harassment through burdensome Freedom of Information Act (FOIA) requests, public inquiries about funding sources, congressional scrutiny, and even direct pressure from outside interests to terminate employment. Academic engagement is an important but risky business.

Yet some scholars decide to engage despite the hazards. In our survey of 330 University of Michigan faculty (see Chapter 7), over 62 percent of respondents give media interviews and 59 percent provide assistance to government agencies. Nearly two-thirds believe that external engagement is complementary to their academic research, although 56 percent feel this activity is not valued by tenure committees and 41 percent consider it to be time consuming and distracting. Roughly 40 percent do not, and never will, use Twitter or Facebook for academic or professional work. Level of engagement appears to be a strong function of the school or department. (Disciplines vary quite widely in their posture toward engagement.) Career stage also makes a difference, with younger faculty expressing more interest in engagement. A Pew Research Center/American Association for the Advancement of Science (AAAS) survey found that 43 percent of 3,748 scientists surveyed believe that it is important for scientists to get coverage for their work in the news media, but 79 percent believe that the news media can't discriminate between well-founded and less unreasonable or illegitimate scientific findings. Forty-seven percent use social media to talk about science, and 24 percent write blogs. Midcareer and older scientists were more likely to speak to reporters; younger scientists were more likely to use social media.[15]

How can we understand the dynamics of these changes and what they mean for the academy as a whole and the scholar as an individual? This report summarizes a three-day meeting that sought to tease the key questions apart. First, what is engagement, and should we do it? This question goes back at least as far as World War II and debates over the role and value of science in society.[16] Today, with an ever-expanding array of ways to engage, even a simple definition of engagement remains unclear. Second, what are the ground rules? Should junior faculty do this? Should this vary by discipline and by school? Should all academics do this? Does this redefine the role of the senior scholar? Third, what are some models that have worked, and what can we learn from them? Fourth and finally, what are the obstacles to engagement, and how can they be overcome?

We are interested in stimulating a dialogue on faculty attitudes and on best practices that cover a span of external engagement activities, including but not limited to congressional testimony, assistance to government agencies, board service, public presentations, media interviews, K–12

---

15. Rainie, L., C. Funk, and M. Anderson. 2015, February 15. *How Scientists Engage the Public.* Washington, DC: Pew Research Center.
16. Kleinman, D. 1995. *Politics on the Endless Frontier: Postwar Research Policy in the United States.* Durham, NC: Duke University Press.

education, blogging, editorial writing, social media, and political activism—all activities that lie outside the "standard" notions of scholarly pursuits.

This meeting and subsequent report were designed to contribute to the ongoing conversation that is taking place in various domains, most notably the National Academies of Sciences' two Sackler Colloquia on "The Science of Science Communication." In all, we had 225 registered participants: 200 from academia, 150 from the University of Michigan, and 50 from other schools. We had representation from 43 disciplines that spanned the physical and social sciences, humanities, and professional schools. This was not a meeting of talking heads. All sessions were arranged as discussions with very brief opening remarks and no PowerPoint slides. This was a working session that led to the document you are now holding. We are very pleased to help advance the conversation about this all-important topic.

2 AGENDA

Wednesday, May 13—*What is the normative problem? What is public and political engagement? Why should we be doing it?*

1:00–1:05	Welcome
	Janet Weiss, Dean, Horace H. Rackham Graduate School, University of Michigan
1:05–1:30	Conference motivation, goals, and agenda
	Andrew Hoffman, Professor and Director, Erb Institute for Global Sustainable Enterprise, University of Michigan
1:30–3:00	Presidents' panel
	Michael Crow, President, Arizona State University
	Philip Hanlon, President, Dartmouth College
	Mark Schlissel, President, University of Michigan
	Teresa Sullivan, President, University of Virginia
	Introduction of President Schlissel: **Katherine White,** Chair, Board of Regents, University of Michigan
	Moderator: **Andrew Hoffman,** Professor and Director, Erb Institute for Global Sustainable Enterprise, University of Michigan
3:00–4:15	Panel 1: Why Should Academics Engage in Public and Political Discourse?
	Brian Baird, President of 4Pir2 Communications; former President, Antioch University Seattle; former US Representative for Washington
	Rachel Cleetus, Lead Economist and Climate Policy Manager, Union of Concerned Scientists

Charles Eisendrath, Director, Knight-Wallace Fellows Program, University of Michigan

Eric Pooley, Senior Vice President for Strategy and Communications, Environmental Defense Fund

Janet Weiss, Dean, Horace H. Rackham Graduate School, University of Michigan

Moderator: **Paul Edwards,** Professor of Information, University of Michigan

4:30–5:15 Breakout 1: What do we mean by public and political engagement?
What pressures are leading us to this discussion? What are considered "appropriate" forms of engagement? Where are the lines between being a content provider and being a political advocate? How do these fit with the types of scholarly engagement advocated by others (such as Roger Pielke Jr.'s *Honest Broker,* or Donald Stokes's *Pasteur's Quadrant*)?

5:15–6:15 Experiences in engagement 1

Juan Cole, Professor of History, University of Michigan

Lisa Nakamura, Professor of American Culture and Screen Arts, University of Michigan

Henry Pollack, Professor Emeritus of Earth and Environmental Science, University of Michigan

Moderator: **Joy Rohde,** Assistant Professor of Public Policy, University of Michigan

7:30–9:00 Public keynote 1: Delivering on Science's Social Contract

Jane Lubchenco, Distinguished Professor of Zoology, Oregon State University, former Administrator of the National Oceanic and Atmospheric Administration (NOAA) and Under Secretary of Commerce for Oceans and Atmosphere

Introduction: **Andrew Maynard,** Professor and Director, Risk Science Center, University of Michigan

Thursday, May 14—*How do we practice public and political engagement?*

8:45–9:00 Welcome and plan for the day
Andrew Hoffman, Professor and Director, Erb Institute for Global Sustainable Enterprise, University of Michigan

9:00–9:30 Steering committee discussion leaders report back on key themes in Breakout 1.
Report back: **Andrew Maynard,** Professor and Director, Risk Science Center, University of Michigan

9:30–10:45 Panel 2: What Are Some Guidelines for Public Engagement?
Nancy Baron, Director of Science Outreach, Communication Partnership for Science and the Sea (COMPASS)

Baruch Fischhoff, Professor of Social and Decision Sciences, Professor of Engineering and Public Policy, Carnegie Mellon University

Roger Pielke Jr., Professor of Environmental Studies, University of Colorado, Boulder

Dan Sarewitz, Co-Director, Consortium for Science, Policy and Outcomes, Arizona State University

Dietram Scheufele, Professor of Life Sciences Communication, University of Wisconsin, Madison

Moderator: **Mark Barteau,** Professor and Director, Michigan Energy Institute, University of Michigan

10:45–11:30 Breakout 2: How does one pursue an academic career that includes public and political engagement? What are the risks and opportunities (both internal and external)? How do they differ by stage of career or discipline? What are the challenges of engagement, including personal, career, and political ones, and what are the options for meeting them? How can one navigate the multiple roles that are part of the engagement process?

12:30–1:00 Steering committee discussion leaders report back on key themes in Breakout 2.

Report back: **David Uhlmann,** Professor and Director, Environmental Law and Policy Program, University of Michigan

1:00–2:15 Panel 3: Models in Practice

Maria Balinska, Managing Editor, The Conversation (US)

Matthew Countryman, Professor and Director, Arts of Citizenship Program, University of Michigan

Michael Kennedy, Director, Science in Society, Northwestern University

Barbara Kline-Pope, Executive Director of Communications, National Academy of Sciences

Amy Schalet, Professor and Director, Public Engagement Project, University of Massachusetts, Amherst

Dawn Wright, Chief Scientist, Environmental Systems Research Institute (Esri), Oregon State University, Aldo Leopold Leadership Fellow

Moderator: **Arthur Lupia,** Professor of Political Science, University of Michigan

2:15–3:00 Breakout 3: What should be the role of academics in public and political discourse? What are the rules of academia and the needs of society, and what should we do if they do not mesh? How can we promote more successful engagement in public discourse? In an increasingly complex and scientifically challenging world, how should we engage the public and the political process? What are the rules of tenure—formal and informal—and how should they change or stay the same? How should young scholars manage their careers in ways that may differ from those of their more senior colleagues?

3:30–4:00 Steering committee discussion leaders report back on key themes in Breakout 3.

Report back: **Lianne Lefsrud,** Postdoctoral Fellow, Erb Institute for Global Sustainable Enterprise, Dow Sustainability Fellow, University of Michigan

4:00–5:00 Experiences in engagement 2

David Uhlmann, Professor and Director, Environmental Law and Policy Program, University of Michigan

Don Boesch, President, University of Maryland Center for Environmental Science

Matthew Davis, Professor of Pediatrics, Professor of Public Policy, University of Michigan

Moderator: **Gregg Crane,** Professor and Director, Program in the Environment, University of Michigan

Friday, May 15—*What are the obstacles to public and political engagement?*

9:00–10:30 Public keynote 2: Good, Bad, and Maybe: Communicating Scientific Near Certainties and Deep Uncertainties to a Nonscientific Audience
Richard Alley, Professor of Geosciences, Pennsylvania State University
Introduction: **Shelie Miller,** Associate Professor, School of Natural Resources and Environment, University of Michigan

10:30–11:45 Panel 4: What Are the Institutional Obstacles, and How Can They Be Overcome?
Dominique Brossard, Professor and Chair, Life Sciences Communication, University of Wisconsin
Susan Collins, Dean, Ford School of Public Policy, University of Michigan
Alison Davis-Blake, Dean, Ross School of Business, University of Michigan
Donald Kettl, Professor and former Dean, School of Public Policy, University of Maryland
David Scobey, Professor and former Executive Dean, The New School for Public Engagement
Moderator: **Barry Rabe,** Professor, Ford School of Public Policy, University of Michigan

11:45–12:30 Breakout 4: What might a playbook for academic engagement in public and political discourse look like? What are the obstacles and incentives for academics to engage in public and political discourse? What are your summary observations from this conference and the topics that it covered?

12:30–1:00 Steering committee discussion leaders report back on key themes in Breakout 4.
Report back: **Shelie Miller,** Associate Professor, School of Natural Resources and Environment, University of Michigan
Closing remarks, next steps, and adjourn

3 SUMMARY REPORT

The Presidents' Point of View

The opening panel included four university presidents in a discussion that tracked the topics of the overall meeting and set the tone for continued discussion. The three themes were why we should engage, how to engage, and how to overcome obstacles to engagement. Although the presidents stressed that the paths to engagement may evolve distinctly among universities, many conclusions were relevant to all.

Why we should engage. President Hanlon (Dartmouth College) summarized three reasons for engagement: (1) we have an obligation to do it, (2) tenure is a privilege that is designed to encourage engagement, and (3) it is necessary for enhancing public debate. President Schlissel (University of Michigan) agreed that "it's actually a responsibility or even an obligation of universities to engage in public discourse and to share the expertise that we accumulate, the knowledge we discover, and the understanding that we achieve with the public at large." Beyond this, he added that tenure should facilitate public engagement: "We forget the privilege it is to have lifelong security of employment at a spectacular university. And I don't think we use it for its intended purpose. I think that faculty on average through the generations are becoming a bit careerist and staying inside their comfort zones." Panelists also felt that the academy should engage to enhance the public debate. In the words of Regent Kathy White (University of Michigan), "Research can only benefit society if we take responsibility for translating this research and inserting it into public discourse." But, warned President Sullivan (University of Virginia), this belief is

> "I think that faculty on average through the generations are becoming a bit careerist and staying inside their comfort zones."—President Schlissel

not universally shared: "There is a fundamental critique among some that we shouldn't be doing research at all—that it's not our mission and that our mission is only teaching. And if you haven't heard that, you haven't been walking the halls of the State Houses lately." Finally, President Schlissel pointed out that engagement is necessary to ensure the relevance and longevity of the university: "If we're perceived as being an ivory tower and talking to one another and being proud of our discoveries and our awards and our accomplishments and the letters after our names, I think in the long run the enterprise is going to suffer in society's eyes and our potential for impact will diminish. The willingness of society to support us will decrease." President Crow (Arizona State University) agreed, but with more urgency: "If we don't figure out how to deal with this—how to teach what theory actually is, how to get people to understand that, how to translate, and how to deal with our tone—the gap between the academic elite and everyone else will continue to grow, and what we now see as political debate will be people with pitchforks outside the door . . . They want to know what we're doing, why we exist, and why they're giving us money. This is a very serious thing that we need to focus on."

> "There is a fundamental critique among some that we shouldn't be doing research at all—that it's not our mission and that our mission is only teaching. And if you haven't heard that, you haven't been walking the halls of the State Houses lately." —President Sullivan

How to engage. In the end, the decision to engage is up to the individual scholar. As President Schlissel explained, "All our schools, all our individual faculty, are free agents. So there's no mechanism to say that we're all going to go this way. Are you kidding me? We can't even get everybody

University presidents from left to right: *Philip Hanlon, Dartmouth College; Teresa Sullivan, University of Virginia; Mark Schlissel, University of Michigan; Michael Crow, Arizona State University*

Andrew Hoffman, University of Michigan (moderator); Teresa Sullivan, University of Virginia; Mark Schlissel, University of Michigan

to show up to a meeting." But, he added, "I think it is a leadership thing and leadership at many different levels. Someone in the president's position or a dean or a chair's position can motivate behavior by celebrating individuals and their successes." Enhancing public debate has become especially pertinent due to the "ubiquity of knowledge" available through social media platforms and new technology. Conversations take place in virtual space; on comment sections of blogs, news sites, and social media; and in online forum sessions. This poses enormous challenges to civil discourse and public dialogue. All four presidents expressed concern with this development. President Hanlon warned that "the real challenge is to focus on the readers . . . If we don't do anything else with our students, we should teach them how complex the world's issues are. We should teach them the difference between anecdote and data." In looking at public debates, President Crow saw confusion more than willful ignorance. To overcome it, he said we need to "articulate the hierarchy of knowledge and explain the way in which knowledge evolves. What's information? What's knowledge? What's know-how? What's not? . . . We need to make sure that people understand that there is a hierarchy to all this and get them to understand it and respect it." President Sullivan added that "there is indeed a big gap between sound bite and nuance . . . I don't think we've got the issue of the gap figured out yet, and maybe there's some new interstitial medium we don't know about yet, or that hasn't been invented yet, that will help us do that." But, she continued, despite this, the insights that social media can provide can help the academy engage. According

> "If we don't do anything else with our students, we should teach them how complex the world's issues are. We should teach them the difference between anecdote and data."
> —President Hanlon

Philip Hanlon, Dartmouth College; Michael Crow, Arizona State University

to President Schlissel, "We need to come to realize that we carry access to the world's information in our pockets, so we don't need to teach students too many facts. We need to teach them how to think and analyze and how to look for facts." He added that social media is "not a gauge of what's true or false or misleading or correct," but it is an "accurate gauge of what people are thinking."

Overcoming obstacles to engagement. According to President Crow, the root of the problem is in the universities themselves. He urged the academy to improve the "Three *T*s"—how we *teach,* how we *translate,* and the *tone* of our discussions. "We are increasingly filled with hubris, filled with arrogance, cut off from the general public, and unable to find an appropriate tone with which to communicate . . . We need to communicate in ways that we've never even thought about before." In addition to working on these skills, increasing diversity was viewed as obligatory. According to President Schlissel, "Unless we can create a milieu here that somewhat replicates the diversity of thought in society, it's going to be very hard for us to work through the problem. So I don't fear our faculty representing themselves and being considered liberal. I'm more concerned that we haven't created a sufficient intellectually and politically diverse

> "I'm more concerned that we haven't created a sufficient intellectually and politically diverse community on our campus."
> —President Schlissel

> "We are increasingly filled with hubris, filled with arrogance, cut off from the general public, and unable to find an appropriate tone with which to communicate."—President Crow

community on our campus." Similarly, changing the culture of the university and the roles of various players within it came to the forefront of the discussion. Moderator Andrew Hoffman (University of Michigan) asked if "we have too many senior professors thinking like junior professors," to which President Crow responded with a call to redefine a role for the full professor: "We're starting to create positions of knowledge curators and educational technology specialists who will be working with our faculty to project their identities and build translation capabilities around them . . . with that, a full professor in this particular world becomes like a super faculty member . . . Scholars don't have the kind of identity in the United States that they have in China and other places, and there are reasons for that that need to be addressed." To help that process along, President Sullivan noted that "you have the right and perhaps the obligation to speak out. And I think our position as administrators is that we have the right and the obligation to protect that when faculty do."

> "You have the right and perhaps the obligation to speak out. And I think our position as administrators is that we have the right and the obligation to protect that when faculty do."
> —President Sullivan

The full transcription of the presidents' panel is in Chapter 5.

Why Should Academics Engage in Public and Political Discourse?

Despite an initial reaction that the question of whether we should engage was in some ways rhetorical, this proved to be a topic that was revisited repeatedly during the conference. In both the panel discussions and breakout sessions, the theme of motivation cut to the heart of the issue: that the academy is facing an existential crisis, and its approach to public and political discourse is fundamental not just to the success of the academy's efforts to connect and engage with society but to its future survival. Many academics approached engagement as a duty, a responsibility born from financial or moral obligations to a public that, via one route or another, funds academic positions and research. Jane Lubchenco (Oregon State University) called engagement part of "scientists' social contract." In the words of Matthew Davis (University of Michigan), "Knowing something is a deflated currency—academia must bridge the 'know' to 'do' gap to be successful and relevant."

Charles Eisendrath (University of Michigan) reminded us that public communication is experiencing a second revolution through social media and changes in the world of publishing, one that is bringing about changes as profound as the first, the invention of the Gutenberg press. Society now has instant access to more news, more stories, more information, more varied formats, and more sources than ever before. For universities to remain relevant, they must learn to engage in a relevant and meaningful way and at a relevant pace. He also added that there are two departments within the university system that are adapting quite effectively to the need for engagement: athletics and development. The scholarly portion of the institution is still lagging.

But Don Kettl (University of Maryland) stressed that this lag is unnecessary, that there is tremendous value in what the academy provides: "In Washington, DC, they are not just hungry for knowledge, for hard facts to inform their decision making; they are famished for it. They

EXPERIENCES IN ENGAGEMENT — MATTHEW DAVIS

Professor of Pediatrics and Communicable Diseases and Professor of Internal Medicine, Medical School; Professor of Public Policy, Gerald R. Ford School of Public Policy, University of Michigan

Matthew Davis, University of Michigan

Dr. Matthew Davis strongly advised people to choose their projects and topics of engagement carefully. When asked how he focuses his work, which includes work in the public sphere as the chief medical executive of the State of Michigan, Davis replied, "For me, the mantra is *relevance*." If the relevance of a project is established early, it is easier to initiate and maintain a meaningful dialogue in the community with which you are working and engaging. An added benefit of such early and focused engagement is that the communication of results and findings from studies becomes easier. Taking the time to understand the needs and questions of the group with which one hopes to work improves the value and accessibility of the completed research, making it of greater value to both policy makers and the public.

Rachel Cleetus, Union of Concerned Scientists; Charles Eisendrath, Director of the Knight-Wallace Fellows Program; Paul Edwards, University of Michigan

Don Kettl, University of Maryland

are looking to us to provide it." But if academics choose not to enter into dialogue with politicians and their advisors, the vacuum will be filled by others with different methods, motives, and positions of authority. In the words of Rachel Cleetus (Union of Concerned Scientists), "If we elect to sit on the sidelines, we allow those with the loudest voices to channel the debate." Many felt that there is a vital role for the academic scholar in public and political discourse, and we must fill it.

Another, perhaps even more powerful, reason for engaging is to excite and inspire, to enthuse a new generation to take up the torch and continue the commitment to inquiry and the pursuit of knowledge in academia. And that will only happen if we can demonstrate the connection between what we do as an institution and its benefit to society.

 **@halpsci**
Why should academics engage? See 7th graders' drawings, before/after @Fermilab visit: http://ed.fnal.gov/projects/scientists/

A little closer to home, some felt that academic engagement can also make the difference in terms of recruitment and retention. If academia does not embrace the opportunity represented by public engagement, it runs the risk of losing the best and brightest young scholars who "want to make a difference" through their work, further reducing diversity in its ranks. This was crystallized by a comment from the floor that academic engagement has a key role to play in embracing underserved populations and addressing the "leaky pipeline" issue. Baruch Fischhoff (Carnegie Mellon University) added that "the intellectual health of our disciplines depends on undertaking this kind of engagement."

Eric Pooley (Environmental Defense Fund [EDF]) recounted the experiences of several EDF researchers who left academia because they sought a deeper engagement in the public policy debate than their university departments encouraged. One left his tenured position at an R1 university in large part because he "was

Baruch Fischhoff, Carnegie Mellon University

fed up with being the one guy in the place whose work was seen as relevant—with relevant being a dirty word." He described another whose department chair was always after him "to 'change up' and do something more theoretical." But Pooley pointed out that new models for engagement allow academics to work alongside nongovernmental organizations (NGOs) on peer-reviewed research that is relevant to public policy, and he held out hope that some researchers would choose to return to the academy after a stint with an NGO to resume scholarly research, enriched by the experience, highly skilled in the art of public engagement, and in a position of strength to promote public and political discourse in their new institution.

@hdabed
Be careful what you wish for @DecisionLab: citing Baruch Fischhoff "Universities are monocultures . . . Pray for pests."

Some graduate students and postdoctoral fellows in attendance—the future generation of academics—expressed frustration with the barriers, disincentives, and discouragement that advisors and departments put in the way of their participation in community engagement activities. And some anticipated that they will vote with their feet. Many did not view the "job for life" represented by tenure as the ultimate goal. In the words of graduate student Andy Henderson (University of Michigan), "There is a distinct willingness in our generation to value public engagement."

> "The younger generation . . . feel[s] keenly invested in being part of the solution, not perpetuating the problem . . . They are seeking ways to have meaningful careers that entail engagement." —Jane Lubchenco

Brian Baird, 4Pir2 Communications; Eric Pooley, Environmental Defense Fund

To that end, some suggested that social media has the power to force change in academia, empowering the next generation that sees scholarship and engagement not as incompatible but rather as two sides of the same coin. If the academy can seize the moment and harness the opportunities for public engagement represented by the media revolution, it can look forward to a strong and vibrant future.

But the demand for more engagement (and interdisciplinary skills) is not coming only from graduate students. Dietram Scheufele (University of Wisconsin) reported that undergraduate students are a driving force for change in educational programming. Barry Rabe (University of Michigan) concurred: "We have a lot to learn from undergraduates. They have been innovative in asking for changes. They are much more interdisciplinary."

Ultimately, though, why an academic makes the choice to engage in public or political discourse is a personal decision, motivated by his or her own circumstances, values, and beliefs and driven by his or her own goals. What makes an oceanographer from California reach out to the surfing community in Malibu, for example, will be very different from the reasons a sociologist connects with an urban regeneration project in Detroit. However, they are united by the desire for the same outcome: to enrich their lives and those of the community they are engaged in and to enrich their own scholarship. Academics who are actively involved in public engagement and working closely with their community tell a similar story to that of Amy Schalet (University of Massachusetts, Amherst), who reported that her experiences have been "incredibly gratifying." Dawn Wright (Esri and Oregon State University) described working with the public as "exhilarating—engaging with a culture that is very different is akin to walking a tightrope." Her sentiment was echoed by many who believe that engagement helps them find meaning and relevance in their own work by placing it in the context of the bigger picture.

Summing up, Jane Lubchenco listed seven major benefits of science most often cited by policy makers: (1) to provide an engine of economic growth, (2) to improve human health and reduce disease, (3) to enable national security, (4) to improve our lives, (5) to enhance national competitiveness, (6) to satisfy innate curiosity, and (7) to inform personal and collective understanding of a variety of issues. Science explains how the world works and how it is changing.

Dawn Wright, Esri and Oregon State University

It suggests likely possible future states, the different paths we can take to reach these states, solutions to the world's problems, and trade-offs of different possible options. To gain the benefits that come from answering these questions, research must be transmitted to the appropriate "public" audience in a timely and effective way.

DELIVERING ON SCIENCE'S SOCIAL CONTRACT
JANE LUBCHENCO

Distinguished Professor of Zoology, Oregon State University, former Administrator of NOAA and Under Secretary of Commerce for Oceans and Atmosphere

Jane Lubchenco, Oregon State University

Drawing on her impressive and varied experiences in academia and government, Dr. Jane Lubchenco spoke about why, when, and how academics should engage with society. An environmental scientist, her talk was illustrated with riveting stories of science communication in particular, but her messages were equally applicable for all academic scholarship. Her practical, insightful advice was liberally punctuated with humor, metaphor, and style—talking the talk while walking the walk.

She began with some thoughts on the role of science in society. When justifying the utility of science today, most people focus on the need to fuel the engine of economic growth, improve health, enable national security, improve our lives, and enhance national competitiveness. But Dr. Lubchenco focused on a less commonly cited reason. Scientific knowledge can inform an understanding of how something works, how it is changing, its likely future states, and the pathways we might take to each. Thus it can identify and evaluate solutions to society's problems. And decisions informed by a scientific understanding are going to be better decisions for both individuals and societies.

Engagement is key to enabling this process: "I'm not suggesting a simplistic 'deficit model' in which an audience is simply an empty vessel that needs filling up with scientific knowledge ... Nor am I talking about science dictating any particular outcome. The concept of 'science to inform, not dictate' explicitly acknowledges that there are multiple factors that will likely affect decisions made by an individual or an institution ... Unfortunately, all too often, scientific knowledge is not at the table, and it's important to ask why."

Scientific information may be lacking because the information is not available to the person who needs it, not understandable, not seen as relevant, or not seen as credible. Many people, including politicians, simply assume that they won't understand what a scientist is saying. And, Dr. Lubchenco explained, "the need for translation is far greater than the current ability of translators to deliver it." Academic scholars have a responsibility to be more proactive in engaging directly with society, creating two-way communication with society. In exchange for public funding, "our jobs are both to create new knowledge and to share it widely with transparency and humility." She called this "scientists' social contract."

So why is engagement not happening more often? Her answer is that academics are ambivalent about public engagement because they fear failure, lack the skills, are uncomfortable with effective tools (such as storytelling, using analogies and metaphors, and talking about themselves), fear that peers will label them as attention seeking, don't want to distract themselves from the things that count in the academic world (namely, publishing and teaching), fear criticism from activists, or believe that public engagement will not be recognized as important and rewarded. But she feels that these legitimate concerns focus on why one should not engage without equal consideration to why or how to do it successfully.

So how can we engage successfully? First, Lubchenco argued that we need to find out where our audience is. Then we need to answer the "so what" question—why should my information be of interest or use to my audience? Key to all this is learning to translate complex scientific concepts and findings into language that is understandable but still accurate and learning to effectively use sound metaphors, analogies, and stories: "Social scientists tell us that stories are sticky. People remember them."

True to her words, Lubchenco told stories that illustrated her advice and demonstrated "knowing what your audience knows and starting from there" and "finding the right analogies." Here are two examples of how she did that:

> Hurricane Sandy triggered a plethora of questions about the relationship between that superstorm and climate change: "Is this a harbinger of things to come? Was Sandy caused by climate change?" I was asked this over and over. Many scientists at the time were answering that question by talking about attribution and the challenges of attributing any single event to climate change. In my experience, when people hear a word like "attribution" that they don't understand, they tune out, distrust the information, or react negatively. So when I was asked that question, I responded with a baseball analogy. I would say, "When a baseball player starts taking steroids, the chances of his hitting home runs suddenly increase dramatically. Not only does he hit more homers, but more powerful ones. Everyone knows one cannot point to any particular home run and say, 'Aha, that home run is because he is taking steroids,' but the pattern that you're seeing of more and bigger homers is understood to be attributable to steroids. In similar fashion, what we are seeing on earth today is weather on steroids—weather on climate steroids. We are seeing more, longer-lasting heat waves, more intense storms, more droughts, and more floods. Those patterns are what we expect with climate change." For many people, that analogy is very helpful.

> I recall one congressional hearing where the topic du jour was the ten-year period of time called the "pause" or the "hiatus" in which we thought there had been no detectable change in the global average temperature. (New information has now shown the hiatus to be an artifact.) And at the hearing, a number of members of the committee asked, "Doctor, isn't it true that the global average temperature of the planet has not changed in the last ten years?" I replied, "Yes, Mr. Representative, that's what the data show." "Well, then, Doctor, isn't it true that climate change isn't happening?" And I replied something like, "Ten years is not a long enough period of time to detect a meaningful trend in a system that's very complex and very noisy." That answer was expected and didn't seem to make any

(continued)

> difference to the questioners. Then I would have another individual ask me pretty much the same question. When a member who I knew was a surfer posed essentially the same question, I tried a different tack. I said to him, "Congressman, have you ever stood on a beach and watched ten waves coming ashore? Could you tell me, based on those ten waves, if the tide was going out or if it was coming in?" And he said, "No, of course not. Ten waves is not enough." Then he became silent, connecting the dots.
>
> Following Dr. Lubchenco's example is an aspirational challenge for many—and worth it. As Dr. Lubchenco concluded, "The topic goes to the heart of the responsibilities of individuals and the academic community to society and how we can best be of service to society."
>
> The full transcription of Jane Lubchenco's keynote is in Chapter 6.

To conclude, one participant (who chose not to pursue a career in academia because of the lack of value placed on public engagement) argued that we should engage with the local community simply because "we are citizens of that community and we should care deeply about it."

How Should Academics Engage in Public and Political Discourse?

The first question asked when discussing public engagement was, who is "the public"—or more accurately, "the publics"—that we are trying to reach? Participants described the publics as a broad range of constituents: consumers of mass media, residents of local communities, politicians, the media, businesses, nonprofits, school groups, and users of medications. Each group requires different modes of engagement. Depending on the audience and the goal of engagement, appropriate information will range from the general to the highly specialized. With a recognition of the diversity of publics and engagement models, multiple themes emerged.

Engagement is a two-way dialogue. Many expressed an uncomfortable realization that our notions of public engagement are based firmly on the deficit model: as "something" that "we" do to "them" to give them the benefit of our knowledge and understanding. It starts with the presumption that "if you knew what I knew, you'd think what I think." Or, as Jane Lubchenco described it, the audience "is simply an empty vessel that needs filling up with scientific knowledge, and then that audience will do whatever the filler-upper would want them to do." This notion is rooted in the (often unconscious) assumption of the superiority of the academy, an assumption that has helped engender the growing estrangement between the academy and the world outside it.

@RogerPielkeJr
Anyone who says that the deficit model of science communication is dead has clearly never been 2 a meeting on science communication

Dawn Wright reminded everyone, "We know it feels good when people listen to us. Now turn that around and think of people who want us to listen." Dan Sarewitz (Arizona State University) added, "The more fun part of the conversation is when we go out and correct wrongs; the more productive part is when we go out and cohabit with people with different belief systems to create solutions to difficult challenges." In this way, Baruch Fischhoff challenged us to "be self-critical and ask, how am I part of the problem that I am trying to solve?"

To this end, participants focused on the extent to which discourse is inherently a dialogue rather than a monologue, a conversation requiring mutual respect and appreciation for the expertise of all sides. Academe needs to accept that it does not have a monopoly on knowledge and expertise and that it is engaging in a two-way learning process. To embark on that process, Dean Janet Weiss (University of Michigan) reminded everyone that academics have an obligation to provide a service to the community—to give value for money and an account of what that money is being used for—but that "academics need to approach public engagement with humility and an awareness that it is not only academe that results in expertise." This is especially true for academics in public universities and, some argued, even more so for land-grant universities. Maria Balinska (The Conversation) added, "The meeting of two worlds often means that both sides are operating outside their comfort zone. Successful communication needs the academic to respect the expertise of the journalist, politician, or citizen."

> "Engagement implies a two-way interaction. It means listening, not just talking."
> —Jane Lubchenco

@JanetEMax
I want to ask: Universities, what kind of neighbor are you? How do you engage w PEOPLE in your city, your region, your state?

This is a model of engagement based on service. Michael Kennedy (Northwestern University) explained, "It starts with four words: 'How can I help?'" adding that we must focus on "listening first and then deploying second." Participants experienced in engagement felt that finding a place where the academic can serve as a resource for an existing community need or initiative is far more successful than the academic trying to impose a certain perspective or approach.

The Honorable Brian Baird (4Pir2 Communications) provoked conversation by stressing how far we may have to stray from our comfort zone to achieve this: "Let me start with a thought, or maybe I should call it a feelings experiment. What if we were to rearrange the title of this meeting? What if instead it read, 'Public and political engagement in academic discourse'?" He paused. "I bet every single one of you cringed at the thought of the public somehow directing and dictating the direction our research should take." A model of genuine engagement entails reaching out to the community and making the effort to discover what issues matter to them, what they need to know, or what help they need so that we can collectively address these issues. In fact, many felt strongly that the academy has as much if not more to learn and gain from its full engagement and integration with society.

> "It starts with four words: 'How can I help?'"
> —Michael Kennedy

Engagement can yield mutual benefit. Matthew Countryman (University of Michigan) pointed out that the goal of engagement is "collaboration with communities to create new knowledge, advancing their knowledge but also engaging public audiences in conversations about the social and public implications of research." Engagement is about creating something that wasn't there before. Whether it is through starting a conversation with the community, supporting new career paths for underserved kids, collaborating with national professional associations, or speaking at the local Kiwanis Club or town hall meeting, engagement ultimately has a beneficial end project or goal for both the academic and the community. For the academic, it can yield better future research questions, a deeper appreciation for the nuanced context in which that research is done, and an expanded network of partners for exploring that context. For the community, it can empower people to offer input and guidance on research that can have an impact on their lives, inform their own decision making with regards to political and social issues, demystify the ivory tower of the academy and those who inhabit it, and expand their own networks for seeking assistance with future issues and challenges. In fact, several participants measured successful engagement by the extent to which it strengthens relationships with those with whom you are engaging. This success is contingent on both parties getting to know each other's goals and needs. But, Michael Kennedy cautioned, the academic cannot merely proclaim, "I'll do whatever the community needs me to do." There is always a deeper set of interests and objectives at play. While community groups and the public are often quick to list their needs and goals, academics must decide how to balance these needs against their expertise, time, and resources. A two-way discussion, wherein both the community and academics mutually develop a project's scope, appropriately sets expectations for both sides. This builds trust and maximizes the likelihood of success for all involved.

Amy Schalet, University of Massachusetts, Amherst; Michael Kennedy, Northwestern University

Dan Sarewitz, Arizona State University

Know your audience. Amy Schalet lamented a point in her career when she realized that if she were to use only the publication channels of her discipline, "there was no way that the knowledge I was producing would reach the people it could help." But the solution was not merely pushing that material out in an unfocused or nondirected way. The general consensus from the meeting was that when it comes to conveying a message to "the public," you must define your audience, learn about them, refine your message, and then develop a strategy to reach them. Barbara Kline-Pope (The National Academy of Sciences) remarked that when our message fails to get through, "the problem is not the audience. The problem is us." In her experience communicating information on energy sources, researchers "needed to learn as much about their audiences as their audiences needed to learn about energy."

Amy Schalet, University of Massachusetts, Amherst

With an audience defined, academics must determine how to appropriately engage with that particular community before people will listen. This is not something that most academics excel at. Nancy Baron (COMPASS) summarized five key points of being a "good communicator," which were reiterated by many at the meeting. First, show your passion—the what, how, and why of what you do. If people are interested *in you*, they will pay attention even if they disagree with you: "Those who show their passion are the most effective." Scientists need to talk not just about what they know but about why they care. Second, do not underestimate the power of being personal. Rather than sticking to the purely objective rationale for a given recommendation, finding, or message, also provide your own personal motivations alongside them. But, she added, the idea of showing passion and being personal can be awkward for some academics: "The idea of actually being passionate about research is a very scary thing for some. It is seen as unscientific."

"Know thy audience, know thyself, know thy stuff—and go forth and enter the fray."
—Nancy Baron, quoting Steven Schneider

Third, find the right stories to make your point, and tell those stories well. Stories are "data with a soul." Many participants reiterated the point that academics must become more adept at storytelling, communicating not just knowledge but also history and context, as well as the personal and persuasive aspects surrounding their research. In their keynote addresses, both Jane Lubchenco and

"I personally think that we need to tell more stories. We need more historians of science and engineering and maybe even engineering more than science—because then people see that the solutions are part of who they are and it's part and parcel of their history."
—Richard Alley

GOOD, BAD, AND MAYBE: COMMUNICATING SCIENTIFIC NEAR CERTAINTIES AND DEEP UNCERTAINTIES TO A NONSCIENTIFIC AUDIENCE   RICHARD ALLEY

Professor of Geosciences, Pennsylvania State University

Richard Alley, Pennsylvania State University

Communicating nuanced, scientific information to general audiences can be a daunting task. However, Dr. Richard Alley challenged attendees to rise to the task of translating research to better inform complex societal issues: "This will be my feeble attempt to show you the value of what you are doing here and why it really shouldn't end here, if at all possible."

Dr. Alley seamlessly wove together colorful humor, history, and science to create a compelling story, one that has long helped him enhance and inform public understanding of climate change. For example, when explaining one problem as early humans began to settle in agrarian societies, he explained, "If you're really sophisticated, you're pooping in your neighbor's drinking water. And if you're not sophisticated, you're pooping in your own drinking water. And there really isn't a third choice." Later in his remarks, tying this same metaphor to climate change, he explained, "If you take all the CO_2 that comes out of our cars in a year and you condense it to the density of horse ploppies and you put it on the roads of America, it's an inch a year. And in a decade, you've got a foot of CO_2 on every road in America, and there are no joggers in America—we're all cross-country skiers!"

Through purposefully placed pictures, graphs, metaphors, and analogies, Alley described with clarity a brief history of world energy production, CO_2 emissions, and agriculture, illustrating how small changes in temperature will dramatically impact agricultural yields across the most vulnerable regions in the word. "This will be a problem," stated Alley, but despite the challenges that climate change presents, he reminded us, "We've got to tell people the good; the story that we can make ourselves better off by dealing with this is not often told very loudly."

Alley believes that stories are powerful mechanisms that can be used to communicate complex science and its relevance in the daily lives of everyday people. To maximize effectiveness, the academy can draw upon the varied expertise of unlikely collaborators and use the voices of other trusted public individuals. Alley recalled, "We learned fantastically from this one project that using different voices really helps. The folks in New York were not blown away by the rear admiral in his dress whites, but the folks in Texas were. And he's telling the same story that I would, but he's telling it way better for a whole lot of people."

He added a note of caution: "We in science have to be very, very good at trying to maintain our own standards and not stepping in the wrong directions or the wrong ways knowing that there is some level of hostility with money that is trying to make us look bad." Quoting Cardinal Richelieu, he added, "Give me six lines in the hand of the most honest of men and I will find something to hang him." But on an optimistic note, we are "starting to see that a Tea Partier might love solar cells for reasons that are very different from the reasons an environmentalist might love solar cells, but they both might love them. So I think there is reason for optimism. I am absolutely convinced that if we say, 'We can't do this,' we will fail. I'm not absolutely convinced that we will succeed. But I'm sure that if we don't try, we will fail. I think we'll succeed."

Looking to the changes necessary within the academy to create more engagement, Dr. Alley identifies the expanding models of what it means to be an academic:

I believe that our triumvirate of teaching, research, and service probably needs to be applied very stringently at the department or college level but may not need to be applied so stringently at the individual level. I suspect that wise administrators are able at some point to say this person is a fantastic teacher, this person is a fantastic researcher, this person is a fantastic outreacher, and we have room for all three of them in the department that is doing teaching, research, and service. So we will have to sneak up on this one carefully. We cannot expect everyone for their entire career to do all three of those at a high level. They're going to find their passion in one direction or another, but recognizing it in the reward structure would be important. And so if there were one thing I could change within the university, it would be the reward structure and how we are defining excellence. We want you to achieve excellence, but I'm not going to define excellence as tightly as I once did.

Richard Alley (Pennsylvania State University) demonstrated their effectiveness at communicating by employing their ability to tell compelling stories that are designed for the particular audience they are addressing—audiences who would otherwise have been closed to their data, models, and jargon.

Fourth, be a leader. Those who lead the herd can get people to pay attention. Fifth, find a community of support that will help you improve. Ultimately, Baron said, "you have to give people something to grab on to if you want them to come with you." Or as Henry Pollack (University of Michigan) pointed out, "How can you craft a message that your audience might be willing to hear?"

An important part of crafting that message lies in the array of tools available to communicate with the public—traditional tools from the mass media (publications, TV and radio broadcasts), public lectures in schools and communities, art and

Roger Pielke Jr., University of Colorado; Nancy Baron, COMPASS

literature, and social media (blogs, Twitter, Facebook, etc.). But often, perhaps under pressure to engage, researchers put the tools before the audience and even the messages. Social media makes this especially easy and prevalent—research groups often create Twitter accounts, Facebook pages, and blogs without a clear audience in mind or message to convey.

Engagement is political and messy. Roger Pielke Jr. (University of Colorado) stated quite firmly that engagement is political whether one acknowledges it or not. Although many academics believe that their work is politically and socially inert—"the data state *x*"—any conclusion that has import for people's beliefs or the way they live their lives will be contested and provocative. As such, the academic cannot control the process by which it is interpreted.

@scheufele
#scicomm is about that "messy space" between values, science and engagement

In the new age of social media and information access, your work may be drawn into the spotlight with or without your consent. Lisa Nakamura (University of Michigan) told participants that they need to take control of their online presence or others will do it for them through Twitter, Facebook, and comment boards, which provide an anonymous means of criticizing, threatening, and otherwise harassing scientists. Juan Cole (University of Michigan) concurred: "If you are out there, this will happen to you, and there is no way to avoid it." In public debate, he warned, opponents will try to make you the issue. In the messiness of public discourse, academics must be able to keep the focus on the issues at hand and be able to distinguish the "trolls from ignorance."

Other participants spoke of similar challenges when engaging with the news media. David Uhlmann (University of Michigan) spoke of the need to be careful about how your views are represented: "It is awful to see your perspective misrepresented or distorted." And, Uhlmann added, this can lead to blowback: "The more public your work, the more potential there is for backlash." Lisa

Left to right: *Lisa Nakamura, Juan Cole, Henry Pollack, and Joy Rohde, University of Michigan*

EXPERIENCES IN ENGAGEMENT — JUAN COLE

Richard P. Mitchell Collegiate Professor of History, University of Michigan

Juan Cole, University of Michigan

Two major influences shaped Dr. Juan Cole's engagement experiences: his early adoption of the World Wide Web and living much of his life in the Middle East. He had a front-row seat to the rise of al-Qaeda while living in Egypt and Pakistan and became well informed on their structure and activity. After the September 11 attacks, he was sought after as one of the few experts on the perpetrators. Dr. Cole initially began blogging simply as a tool to organize archived e-mails. But soon this tool became a standalone fixture for communicating real-time reports from local communities affected by both al-Qaeda and the US-led war on terrorism. He translated Arabic news articles published in small towns all over the Middle East, and before he knew it, he had a million page views: "I had never had a million of anything. I think my best-selling book up to that point had sold 560 copies from Princeton University Press."

Dr. Cole's experiences in engagement demonstrate how Internet technology has enhanced the scholar's ability to engage meaningfully and in real time with interested members of the public. Had Cole sought to share his knowledge about on-the-ground events during the Gulf War, for example, he would have faced long lead times as he gathered print media sources. Furthermore, he would have had to convince major media outlets like the *New York Times* to publish his work.

But blogging has allowed him to reach more people and has widened his depth of knowledge and areas of interest. He was also singled out by Vice President Biden (then minority leader) to speak to the Senate Foreign Relations Committee because it was not satisfied with the information that the White House was providing. However, Dr. Cole did caution that engaging in this way has not always been easy. Once you join the discussion, he warned, you may face criticism, personal attacks, and trolling. But, Dr. Cole told the audience, "if you stick to your guns, and you try to make sure what you are saying is as well grounded as possible, over time you can have an impact in public discourse."

Nakamura pointed out that media engagement is becoming more challenging. Journalists, for example, are now seeking press requests using social media and will listen to whoever responds first. However, she cautioned the audience to spend the extra time to do their homework before consenting to an interview. Uhlmann offered two strategies. First, begin conversations on "background." This will offer your perspective without being directly quoted. Second, prepare sound bites ahead of time. Reporters not only will oblige but will appreciate this because they want your help and perspective, and they want it efficiently. In

David Uhlmann, University of Michigan

the end, Uhlmann was encouraging: "You should not shy away from research in areas of public interest if it something that drives you." But one key strategy for reducing the messiness of engagement is preparation.

Training, formal and informal. Another key strategy is training, both early and ongoing. First, many participants felt that training should start early, as part of the curricular or cocurricular training of doctoral students. One example is the Researchers Expanding Lay-Audience Teaching and Engagement (RELATE) program, which was started at the University of Michigan in 2013 by a group of graduate students as a way of helping "graduate students and early career researchers develop stronger communication skills and actively facilitating a dialogue between researchers and different public communities." The importance of early training in engagement also relates to the longer-term prospects that scholars will engage in later in their career. As one participant noted, "If a faculty member spends little time on outreach activities pretenure, we cannot expect them to 'flip a switch' and be able to engage once given tenure." Second, many felt that training should be an ongoing part of an academic's career—for postdoctoral fellows, assistant professors, associate professors, and full professors. Barbara Kline-Pope pointed out that absent such continuous learning, "people fall back into their comfort zones." This training, no matter which stage in one's career, can be both formal and informal.

@Nancy_Baron
How do you have a positive media experience? Prepare. Work out your sound bites. @UMichLaw Yes! The sound bite is your friend

Formally, universities see increasing value in hiring public relations professionals to aid academics in their engagement pursuits. University press offices can help with the preparation of media releases, provide education and training, and help increase the visibility of individual scholars to the benefit of both that scholar and the institution as a whole. Academics should be aware of these internal resources and seek them out in the event that they are thrust into the twenty-four-hour cable news cycle or put under attack on social media. Utilizing these services, however, is not limited to defensive action. Academics who wish to communicate their research to those outside their field should work with their public relations departments to discuss the best routes of dissemination and seek guidance on message and narrative.

Whether internal training in communication skills becomes a mainstay for academics depends greatly on the institution and department, but some universities have moved to specifically target training in engagement and communication. The University of Wisconsin–Madison, for example, has created the Department of Life Sciences Communication, which grants doctorate degrees as well as communication minors for bench scientists. Dietram Scheufele reported that the first offering of a course on science, media, and society attracted one hundred interested students from five different colleges.

Barbara Kline-Pope, National Academy of Sciences

EXPERIENCES IN ENGAGEMENT — LISA NAKAMURA

Gwendolyn Calvert Baker Collegiate Professor of Screen Arts and Cultures and American Cultures, University of Michigan

Lisa Nakamura, University of Michigan

Dr. Lisa Nakamura's engagement experiences have increased alongside public interest in her research topic. This past year, the public has grown particularly hungry for information regarding harassment of female video game developers and female video game players. Since 1994, Dr. Nakamura has been studying how people identify each other when it comes to race and gender during their interactions in online video games. What was once considered an obscure topic has placed her in the spotlight and under criticism by "some of the most unkind, uncivil people you can possibly imagine: online 24/7 video game players." Her audience is no longer restricted to academic circles, and she advised that "if you don't have your hand on the wheel of your own public image and how your research comes across, someone else will." She explained that social media has changed public engagement profoundly and that many of her talks have ended up on YouTube or shared on Twitter without her consent.

But Dr. Nakamura also warned that the challenges of engagement for women and people of color include disparities in access to engagement. For example, she pointed out the extent to which access to mainstream media, the academic's established route to the public, is not equal across gender and race. The media will typically look for white males to represent the authority on any given subject.

Beyond the individual institution, there is a growing array of training platforms available to the individual scholar. For example, the Leopold Leadership Program at Stanford University's Woods Institute for the Environment provides resources and training for midlevel academics, covering topics like building and leading teams, working with Congress, and communicating through print and social media. Its sister program, COMPASS, provides training, individual coaching, and networking opportunities to help academics participate more effectively in public discourse about the environment.

Another avenue for engagement training that many academics automatically participate in is the act of writing the significance statement or "broader impacts" discussion when applying for grant funding or submitting a publication. These practical opportunities are essentially a feedback loop. Don Boesch (University of Maryland) explained that not only do these pieces help young faculty and trainees become better at crafting their message, but when executed well, they can set applicants apart in the funding arena.

Moving to the more informal modes of training, participants talked about finding role models and mentors. They encouraged participants struggling for support and training to look to those who have already been involved to learn directly from their personal experience. As the domain

Matthew Davis, University of Michigan; Don Boesch, University of Maryland

of academic engagement is still undefined, learning from direct experience can be invaluable. While many universities are stretched for resources and working with limited budgets, Dean Susan Collins (University of Michigan) noted that instead of competing against one another for recognition, academics may have a greater impact if they find ways to collaborate across institutions.

Finally, many participants and panelists stressed that audiences can be one of the best resources for engagement training. By actually engaging and then seeking feedback from those with whom they have engaged, scholars can develop their own experience that is personally tailored to their own communication style and the audiences they seek to engage. Further, engaging with communities outside their regular audiences can help scholars develop a more diverse set of skills.

Entering the world of politics. Finally, while all types of academic engagement are inherently political, the true political nature of academic research becomes evident when scholars offer testimony or advice to elected officials at local, state, and national levels. During the conference, two distinct views emerged on the potential role of academics within this arena. One focused on how the world of politics and policy needs the wisdom and insight of the academic world; the other articulated the hegemonic role of the political sphere, arguing that academics must enter the political arena with deference. However, advocates of either standpoint agreed that academics need to learn specialized skills for addressing political audiences.

The reasons for believing that academics can offer uniquely valuable insights for informing policy were based on the value of what they produce—the data, results, and conclusions they create—as well as the models and analytical rigor utilized in the process. Several panelists argued that academics can help inject a valuable dose of nuance and appreciation of the inherent complexity of pressing social and environmental issues. Matthew Davis suggested that there is a great hunger for policy-relevant science, but few scientists are looking to address the questions that policy makers are grappling with. In his words, "When science is sidelined in policy debates, some of that responsibility comes back to the academy." There is a need for scientists and researchers to think about policy relevance and interact with political actors to help inform their research agenda.

@2020science
"Politics is the way we get done the business of living together"—don't diss politics @RogerPielkeJr

On the other side, several panelists argued that the political world trumps the academic world and that academics should enter the political world with appropriate expectations. Roger Pielke Jr.

Dietram Scheufele, University of Wisconsin

argued that academics must hold a theory of their political value before entering into policy debates. He argued that it is impossible to impart the values of the academy into the political sphere: "Politics is bigger and stronger than anything we can bring to bear there." He advocated for academics to expand the scope of political debates by including all relevant information and varied voices and perspectives. Other panelists made similar observations; even when facts are agreed upon, the interpretation of those facts and how they should inform policy will be very different for different political actors. Dietram Scheufele noted that all people, including academics, tend to have motivated reasoning and confirmation bias, and as such, few policy debates are truly about narrow questions of science or fact. For these panelists, it is not the appropriate role of academics to "save" politics from its worst offenses relative to academic values. Rather, academics must enter in political contexts with a fuller understanding of their essentially secondary role.

In the end, panelists argued strongly that the most powerful and direct impact that an academic can have through his or her research is through the political realm. Therefore, the development of skills to

work in this arena is critical for any kind of engagement strategy or training. These skills are different from those for engaging with the news media and the general public.

How Can Institutional Obstacles to Engagement Be Overcome?

The broad range of participants in the meeting, from graduate students to deans to university presidents, agreed that the academy is currently ill-prepared to support faculty in their efforts to engage in public discourse. President Crow pointed out that the public is starved for information, but the academy does a poor job at translating its knowledge into a "usable form." However, many also saw encouraging signs that things were changing. Though much needs to be done, the conversation focused on three primary topics: tenure, career development, and faculty culture.

Support for faculty engagement must send the clear message that such activities are valued. While recognition dinners and other activities that an institution can use to influence its faculty were mentioned, the power of tenure was a recurrent theme in discussions, both as a source of resistance and as a lever for change.

As a source of resistance, President Sullivan and others noted that the institution of tenure makes faculty members conservative and careerist in their approach toward research. Participants agreed that faculty members eschew engagement, since it is not highly valued in the areas of tenure evaluation: research, teaching, and service. But as a lever of change, reward structures must be changed so that faculty members are incentivized and honored, not penalized, for adding this dimension to their academic identity. Dominique Brossard (University of Wisconsin) put it succinctly: "You know what works in faculty engagement? The carrot and the stick."

> "If there were one thing I could change … it would be the reward structure and how we are defining excellence. We want you to achieve excellence, but I'm not going to define excellence as tightly as I once did."
> —Richard Alley

Participants raised the question of whether a change in tenure rules should be addressed at the departmental, school, or institutional level. The university presidents indicated that tenure evaluations need to be addressed in a bottom-up fashion, as each department or faculty has its own agenda, while some participants expressed the belief that signaling from higher levels of administration would quicken the pace of change.

Many stressed that the goal should not be to change the definition of the academic scholar such that all must engage. Instead, the goal should be to widen the range of definitions of what it means to be an academic scholar, allowing more diversity within our ranks. As Andrew Maynard (University of Michigan) warned, "There is a range of career paths that students will follow, but we do not have structures to teach skills for multiple career paths."

Dominique Brossard, University of Wisconsin

Participants also indicated that an increase in participation in public engagement is coming from student demand. The newest generation of students—both graduate and undergraduate—wishes to use their academic credentials to tackle complex, "real-world" problems. This demand is encouraging universities with "traditional" research infrastructures to offer more outreach activities, such as social entrepreneurship programs, outreach initiatives, and problem-specific centers.

Ultimately, the fundamental challenge according to David Scobey (The New School for Public Engagement) is that a change in the overall faculty culture must occur, moving away from the marginalization and contempt of faculty engagement toward a culture where these kinds of work are valued at a level

 @JoyRohde
Must recognize how our homogeneity constrains genuine engagement

more equal to the traditional activities of research and publication. Don Kettl supported the need for a cultural redirection by challenging the notion that faculty whose engagement outweighs

David Scobey, The New School for Public Engagement; Barry Rabe, University of Michigan

their publication record cannot be tenured. He argued that this kind of thinking is out of date and does not allow space for the increased value that public and political engagement offers the scholar and the institution.

But signs of change are visible. Several panelists offered examples of ways that their institutions have begun to enhance the value of academic engagement by their faculty. In response to the growing gap between business school research and company needs, Dean Alison Davis-Blake (University of Michigan) noted that the Ross School of Business has added "practice" as a fourth category to their tenure review process with the goal of encouraging faculty to work on problems that have real value to private-sector business practitioners. But she warned that academia is a competitive market where faculty members act as free agents. If one school establishes idiosyncratic metrics for tenure, an untenured junior faculty member would be unwise to follow them unless they were guaranteed tenure. The risk of a resume that is not valued by the broader market is too great. To take some of the burden and risk off her faculty, Susan Collins explained that the Ford School of Public Policy has hired people with experience in communicating scholarly work to assist faculty who wish to engage in public and political spheres.

> "How do we assess the quality of engagement activities? This is something we should grapple with. Developing a peer review or other approach for assessing quality would enable us to consider folding engagement into an academic promotion system." —Susan Collins

Despite such efforts to reward and support engagement, the issue of how to quantify and assess the quality of this work remained an area of debate. The peer review process has been well vetted as a means of evaluating the impact of academic research, but this does not readily translate to the assessment of the impact of a faculty member's engagement-based work. President Sullivan wondered, and Dominique Brossard stressed, that new forms of social media analytics will most likely play a role in quantifying impact in a way that is as rigorous as peer review. Another solution that was proposed was more flexibility in determining who is a peer or colleague in the tenure review process. A junior faculty member

 @brossardd
"We got 1 million views on Youtube and 4 million on PBS. In other words, nobody saw us"—How do you evaluate success?

who has performed public or political engagement should be evaluated by a peer who has also conducted this type of work, rather than one who is only aware of scholarly merit. With the right combination of changes to the tenure criteria, review process, and departmental support, universities can create a climate where faculty can feel comfortable and incentivized to engage with the public and political sectors.

Susan Collins and Alison Davis-Blake, University of Michigan

The Students' Point of View

A recurring theme throughout the meeting was the generational shift currently taking place within academia, with younger students and faculty seeking different prospects, aspirations, and skills than their more senior colleagues. With roughly one-third of the academic participants in this meeting comprising PhD and postdoctoral students, there was much discussion among them in panel sessions, breakout groups, and sidebar conversations.[17]

Many graduate students and early career researchers attending the meeting agreed that their generation placed a high value on engagement. But many went further, saying that they had chosen a research career precisely because they wanted to contribute to the real world, to offer their knowledge and expertise in order to make a difference. And, as Sarah Wilson warned, if academia doesn't value engagement, and indeed discourages it "by placing so many obstacles in our path, then we will choose to follow a different route." This echoed a concern expressed by others—that people who value engagement will either leave academia because there is, in the words of one participant, "no space for them in the traditional mold," or gravitate toward schools that reward such behavior, creating a variable of differentiation among universities.

And the obstacles are certainly many. Jane Lubchenco pointed out that even faculty who engage successfully often advise their grad students against it or at least caution that they defer it until they have achieved tenure. Academia is still focused on the narrow goal of tenure, a topic that came up repeatedly during the meeting, often to the frustration of student attendees, with Sarah Wilson commenting, "At this point, tenure is not even on the table; we just want a job." A sentiment felt by many of the students present was that the majority of them will never come up for tenure, whether through choice or the academy's filtering process. Despite this, career guidance from most faculty advisors consists of "publish, publish, publish," with any form of "service" activity discouraged as time that

> **@epuckett**
> Being a #librarian gives me more flexibility to do community engagement than a career in academia

---

17. Some graduate and postgraduate students preferred to remain anonymous in their comments.

Arthur Lupia, Peter Goldberg, and Andy Henderson, University of Michigan

could have been better used to produce another paper. The frustration is such that many no longer tell their advisors that they are involved in any form of public engagement. They felt that some means of evaluating their worth beyond their number of publications needed to be established.

However, focusing on the current barriers risks overlooking the opportunities that this generation gap presents. Many early career participants felt that their generation has the skills required to communicate with the public in the public's arena of choice: social media. It is easier than ever before to reach a wide audience, to join and inform discussion, to disseminate knowledge, and to reach out to communities using the widening array of social media tools. And for those who do seek tenure, Arthur Lupia (University of Michigan) speculated that "social media is going to redefine metrics for the next generation of scholars." President Sullivan argued that "the difficulty with Twitter or Facebook being accepted as credible is that you don't have a quality apparatus, something like peer review, currently available for that." Many young scholars felt that social media platforms have already established novel analytics to assess the impact of social media—analytics that can be refined to focus on the impact on selective demographics, providing a far more powerful and insightful measure than the current set of metrics.

Mark Barteau (University of Michigan) believed that "PhD students have an opportunity to engage because they have the time to really focus on a single project for an extended period of time," and they bring to that task a real desire to communicate widely about that project. He noted that new students have been more "innovative in requesting change," far more interdisciplinary in their work, and

@AvastMachine
Academics stuck in words while living in a world (incl our students) that craves/creates video!

far more willing to work "outside their comfort zones." Many participants felt that the academy will have to change as this generation matures in their fields, regardless of whether it chooses to. But they felt, given that pending reality, a more efficient and effective way to bring about the needed changes would be to institute training now and help shape the changes already under way in graduate student behavior. If the academy is willing to train the next generation in an ability to listen and to engage in genuine conversation, Gregg Crane (University of Michigan) felt that graduate students will "affect change in a way the current generation" that is leading academia cannot, thereby helping secure the future of the academy.

Imagining the Future of Public and Political Engagement

"A good meeting is one that challenges you and leaves you more uncertain at the end, that forces you to think about the issues," concluded Andrew Maynard. And by that account, this was a successful meeting. While universities are facing increasing pressure to engage in political and social discourse, many questions were left unanswered and ways forward left undetermined. While many observed that a sense of urgency on this topic is not sufficiently understood within the broader academy, those present felt strongly that engagement was critical to our future. Arthur Lupia warned, "If we want to be relevant in the public sphere, we have to step up our game, because we lost the monopoly on communication." If we do not, we will be absent in public and political discourse, which could lead to greater restrictions in public support of universities to create, test, and disseminate knowledge.

Andrew Maynard, University of Michigan

However, throughout the meeting, participants expressed a variety of examples of ways in which the academy is indeed changing for the better. Not only is the desire for discourse increasing, particularly among more junior academics, but opportunities and institutional support for engagement are also growing. Some universities are becoming more aware and inclusive of diverse opinions that exist within and outside their walls and are striving to be more relevant by breaking their isolation in their ivory towers. For President Crow,

> @brossardd
> The scholar of tomorrow has to be engaged PERIOD, or it's a problem for all of us.

one of the things that we need to do in this moment of time is to define what university means to us. In our case, we're reconceptualizing the university to be a knowledge enterprise. We produce knowledge, synthesize knowledge, store knowledge, and analyze knowledge, and the three things that we produce from that process are people, ideas and concepts, and things and objects. A lot of places that call themselves universities don't do that. So we have got to find some way to recapture the term, the idea of what we actually are, because that's all being corrupted as we speak.

The manifestation of that effort is the growing array of efforts taking place at individual universities and the broader academy to facilitate this process.

Further, academic publishers are introducing more practitioner-oriented journals for disseminating articles written with real-world applications that are tailored to a broader audience. Professional organizations are arranging more conferences that span the boundaries of academia and practice, facilitating meetings between academics and policy makers, and developing platforms to allow academics and stakeholders to exchange points of view and explore common areas of interest. Academic scholars have access to more career options that straddle academia and the worlds of politics, education, and media. Similarly, new occupations, such as science communicator, are emerging on university campuses. Traditional tenure and reward structures are beginning to include engagement as a fourth activity, alongside research, teaching, and service. And there is an increasing array of specialized programs to teach and research issues around science communication (see Chapter 4).

But much more still needs to be done. Participants agreed that two issues are paramount. First, engagement must be included in rewards and incentives across the entire academy. This is an institutional issue, not one restricted to an individual school or department. Incentive schemes (such as prizes, awards, and fellowships) and training programs should be further developed to encourage researchers to engage with the wider community from the outset of their careers. Social media must be fully utilized both to disseminate research and also to measure its true impact.

Second, more research might be conducted to clarify the "rules of the game," articulating how academics can and should incorporate public engagement into their careers. There is much that we still do not know about this activity: How might the rules of engagement differ by discipline? What role should the academic scientist play in public and policy debates? What is considered legitimate engagement, and where is the boundary between knowledge source and knowledge advocate? What are the skills necessary for engagement, and what best practices exist for engagement? How does engagement alter publication strategy? What are the multiple roles in the science communication process, and how can we construct a rich and diverse typology that expands our notions of what it means to be an academic scholar? When should academics begin to include engagement in their portfolio of activities? How should they phase it over the span of their career? In the words of Mark Barteau, "When do you have enough stature to engage? That depends on where you are, what your field is, the vehicle of engagement, and your audience."

Mark Barteau, University of Michigan

Participants and conference conveners discussed the possible value of creating a handbook or guide that articulates some ground rules for academic engagement. Yet many concluded that such a guidebook might be elusive. As Shelie Miller (University of Michigan) reminded us, "What are the rules of engagement? There aren't any. I don't think it is possible to distill all the variables into a single set of rules for engagement. And that's not a bad thing." The next challenge is to create greater clarity in this nascent domain.

4 RESOURCES FOR ACADEMIC ENGAGEMENT IN PUBLIC AND POLITICAL DISCOURSE

Development and Training Opportunities

- American Association for the Advancement of Science (AAAS) Center for Public Engagement with Science and Technology, http://www.aaas.org/pes
- AAAS Communicating Science Workshops, http://www.aaas.org/pes/communicating-science-workshops
- AAAS Dialogue on Science, Ethics, and Religion, http://www.aaas.org/DoSER
- AAAS Leshner Leadership Institute for Public Engagement with Science, http://www.aaas.org/pes/leshner-leadership-institute
- AAAS Mass Media Science and Engineering Fellows Program, http://www.aaas.org/program/aaas-mass-media-science-engineering-fellows-program
- Barefoot Challenge of Science Leadership, http://www.barefoot-thinking.com/scientists.html
- COMPASS, http://www.compassonline.org
- ComSciCon, Harvard University, http://comscicon.com
- Global Young Academy, http://globalyoung.academy
- Leopold Leadership Program, Stanford and Duke Universities, https://leopoldleadership.stanford.edu
- Life Sciences Communication Department, University of Wisconsin, http://lsc.wisc.edu
- Public Engagement Project, University of Massachusetts, Amherst, https://www.umass.edu/pep/
- Science in Society Program, Northwestern University, http://scienceinsociety.northwestern.edu
- Union of Concerned Scientists Science Network Workshop Series, http://www.ucsusa.org/action/science_network/science-network-workshop-series.html#.VYredPlVikp

- Wilburforce Foundation, Fellowship in Conservation Science, http://www.wilburforce.org/fellowship

Assistance in Reaching Broader Publics

- AAAS Mass Media Science and Engineering Fellows Program, http://www.aaas.org/program/aaas-mass-media-science-engineering-fellows-program
- AAAS Science and Technology Policy Fellowships, http://www.aaas.org/program/science-technology-policy-fellowships
- American Chemical Society Public Policy Fellowship Programs, http://www.acs.org/content/acs/en/policy/policyfellowships/programs.html
- Arts of Citizenship Program, University of Michigan, http://artsofcitizenship.umich.edu
- Citizen Alum, http://www.citizenalum.org
- The Conversation (US), https://theconversation.com/us/
- Imagining America, http://imaginingamerica.org
- Intergovernmental Platform on Biodiversity and Ecosystem Services, http://www.ipbes.net
- Macmillan Science Communication, http://msc.macmillan.com
- NASA Science Mission Directorate Scientist Speakers' Bureau, http://www.lpi.usra.edu/education/speaker/
- National Academies of Science Christine Mirzayan Science and Technology Policy Graduate Fellowship Program, http://sites.nationalacademies.org/PGA/policyfellows/index.htm
- National Academy of Sciences, Science and Engineering Ambassadors Program, http://scienceambassadors.org/about/
- Researchers Expanding Lay-Audience Teaching and Engagement (RELATE), University of Michigan, http://www.learntorelate.org
- Scholars Strategy Network, Harvard University, http://www.scholarsstrategynetwork.org

Research and Education

- Alan Alda Center for Communicating Science, http://www.centerforcommunicatingscience.org
- Belfer Center for Science and International Affairs, Science, Technology, and Policy Program, Harvard University, http://belfercenter.ksg.harvard.edu/project/44/science_technology_and_public_policy.html
- FemTechNet, http://femtechnet.org
- National Academies of Science, Arthur M. Sackler Colloquia 2012, *The Science of Science Communication I,* http://www.nasonline.org/programs/sackler-colloquia/completed_colloquia/science-communication.html
- National Academies of Science, Arthur M. Sackler Colloquia 2013, *The Science of Science Communication II,* http://www.nasonline.org/programs/sackler-colloquia/completed_colloquia/agenda-science-communication-II.html
- University of Toronto Science Leadership Program, http://www.provost.utoronto.ca/public/pdadc/2014_to_2015/55.htm

5 PANEL DISCUSSION: PRESIDENTS CROW, HANLON, SULLIVAN, AND SCHLISSEL

ANDREW HOFFMAN, MODERATOR: Good afternoon. In this session we have, in alphabetical order, Michael Crow, President of Arizona State University; Phil Hanlon, President of Dartmouth College; Mark Schlissel, President of the University of Michigan; and Teresa Sullivan, President of the University of Virginia. Each will offer three minutes of opening remarks, and then we will move to a moderated discussion followed by questions from the audience.

PRESIDENT CROW: The public and political debate associated with climate change is a perfect example of the imperative for academic engagement. In this context, I wrote down three words that all start with the letter *T*. The first is teaching. We need to convey to students the complexity of issues like climate change, but we do not yet know how to teach what a theory entails and how theories evolve. What we understand now is less than and different from what we will understand at some point in the future. As mentioned in the opening comments, people do not grasp what we do. Second, translation—we're terrible translators. We have scientists in the climate change debate standing up and saying that the earth is going to end—that if we do not take action in the next few months, the fate of all of humanity will be altered. Maybe, but probably not, and certainly not with that tonality. It is difficult not to remember that just ten thousand years ago, where the Empire State Building sits today, there was a thousand feet of ice, and that was long before we were doing what we're doing. So I'm just saying, we're really bad translators. And the last is our tone—our tonality as teachers. We are increasingly filled with hubris, filled with arrogance, cut off from the general public, and unable to find an appropriate tone with which to communicate. And so I would suggest that the fantastic thing about us getting together here today to talk about academic engagement and public and

From left to right: *Andrew Hoffman, University of Michigan (moderator); Teresa Sullivan, University of Virginia; Mark Schlissel, University of Michigan; Philip Hanlon, Dartmouth College; Michael Crow, Arizona State University*

political discourse is that we need it more than we've ever needed it. We need to communicate in ways that we've never even thought about communicating before, because if we don't figure out how to deal with this—how to teach what theory actually is, how to get people to understand that, how to translate, and how to deal with our tone—the gap between the academic elite and everyone else will continue to grow, and what we now see as political debate will be people with pitchforks outside the door. Pitchforks! They want to know what we're doing, why we exist, and why they're giving us money. This is a very serious thing that we need to focus on.

PRESIDENT HANLON: Let me first say that this is a very important topic, and I want to thank the organizers for inviting me. I want to speak just for a minute about the "why" part of what we are discussing. Should academics be engaged in public debate, and if so, why? And I think that it's not only a good thing; it's actually an obligation that we do so. I have picked three different reasons. The first is that the public invests a lot in higher education through research funding, federal loans, and state appropriations. It's never as much as we think it should be, but nonetheless it adds up to a very large number, and so we have an obligation to give back the fruits of our labor. Number two is tenure. We think of tenure as a right, but it's really a privilege: the privilege to be able to explore whatever you want, whatever topics you think are important or interesting, and I think that privilege comes with a ton of responsibilities to share with the public at large the fruits of what we discover. Number three is the biggie. The world's issues are incredibly complex and public debate is, from all evidence, deteriorating. Incredibly complicated topics are being reduced to sound bites of very shallow analysis. We have an opportunity to set a model for our students, and we want our graduates to leave here and understand the complexity of the world's issues and that the power of the mind is the best tool we all have to overcome them. And so we can set a model for our students by engaging ourselves in public debate and, as great as we are collectively and as great as the research we do on campus is, the biggest tool we have to change society is our graduates: the really bright minds that run through our place and go out. If we prepare them correctly, if we model behavior for them correctly, if we model engagement for them, they will become passionate and they will engage in deep, profound public debate instead of just trivial debate.

PRESIDENT SCHLISSEL: Thank you for this opportunity. This is great and I'm particularly excited to be sitting here with my colleagues. So I share with my fellow presidents the notion that it's actually a responsibility or even an obligation of universities to engage in public discourse and to share the expertise that we accumulate, the knowledge we discover, and the understanding that we achieve with the public at large. And I'm speaking at an institutional level, so that means that it's not every individual's personal responsibility; it's really up to the individuals to choose, but as an institution and as presidents, we help shape the culture and the value system as well as reflect that culture and value system. I think, as an institution, it really is part of our obligation to society for the reasons that Phil [Hanlon] has mentioned. I think this engagement has a pretty significant effect on how the public at large thinks about us. So we're not quite dragging them to the front doorstep with pitchforks, but if we're perceived as being an ivory tower and talking to one another and being proud of our discoveries and our awards and our accomplishments and the letters after our names, I think in the long run the enterprise is going to suffer in society's eyes, and our potential for impact will diminish. The willingness of society to support us will decrease. So really, the engagement piece is part of how the public sees us, and that is actually a double-edged sword.

Anybody who works at this university can certainly identify himself or herself as a professor of the University of Michigan, and their public engagement will reflect on our entire community. But it really can be messy; we are a community that values freedom of expression and freedom of thought for what we choose to study and how we choose to represent ourselves. We get accused, for example, of being a bastion of liberal thinking, and that can be reinforced depending on who's speaking out and how. So it's not going to be a pure win every single time professors from the university speak in public or interpose themselves. But the act of being engaged is critical for the public's perception of our value. That spectrum of engagement ranges from individual scholars offering knowledge, expertise, and data information that they have to being advocates for a policy, conclusion, perspective, or outcome that they're seeking to put into the marketplace of ideas, all the way to actively participating in politics. There are politicians who were professors and some people who are temporary politicians with links to the academy. So there's a very broad spectrum, and I think we're on the safest ground when we speak as subject matter experts, but it's not quite that simple. I think all of us as individuals—whether you're a professor, a staff member, or a student—have a right to speak out in public; you have a right to express your personal views. But I think that with those rights come responsibilities. You have to realize that the audience isn't going to distinguish between your personal views and those of the institution as a whole. We had a little to-do about this here at Michigan in my first semester when one of my colleagues submitted an op-ed at an online venue. The editorial writer titled it "Why I Hate Republicans," and we're off to the races. We allow freedom of expression, but it led to a piling on of those who wanted to take cheap and easy shots at the quality and the nature of thought in teaching. Then it has a second downside that I think we ought to

be very sensitive to as teachers. If our students perceive us as having a powerful point of view, that may suppress students from speaking or developing their own points of view; it's a polarizing relationship. I don't want a kid in my class to be afraid to write something in an essay that disagrees with me because he or she might not get a good grade. So it's complicated, and it requires sensitivity and caution, and certainly while we're expressing political beliefs, I think caution is definitely required.

Finally, I want to agree with what Dr. Crow said about the tenure issue. We don't appreciate it, and we forget the privilege it is to have lifelong security of employment at a spectacular university. And I don't think we use it for its intended purpose. I think that faculty on average through the generations are becoming a bit careerist and staying inside their comfort zones. Once we get that tenure, we can keep doing just what it is that got us here. And I think if there is a purpose to tenure moving forward, it really is to free us up to take on challenging problems, to engage in public discourse without having this existential worry that we'll be expressing a view before its time or a view out of the mainstream.

PRESIDENT SULLIVAN: I also want to thank the organizers for allowing me to come back to Michigan. The Michigan meetings are a wonderful idea, and I'm glad to have an opportunity to participate in this one. Could I see a show of hands again for those of you who are graduate students? Thank you. I thought about my remarks with graduate students in mind, and I guess one of the reasons for this is that my older son became an assistant professor for the first time last fall. So he is teaching comparative religion in a public university in Texas. What could go wrong? [Laughter] Watching the academy through his eyes, I see one set of issues, and I've had my own experiences, too. Shortly after I arrived at the University of Virginia, we were served with a civil discovery order by the attorney general, which is something like a lawsuit, demanding that we produce all the e-mails our climate scientists had written to each other and to a long list of other climate scientists. We resisted this and said we thought this was a misinterpretation of the state's laws. The attorney general, unfortunately, is also my lawyer. So I expressed the opinion that I didn't wish him to be both prosecuting and defending me at the same time. He expressed surprise that I thought he couldn't do that and that I had to have permission from him to hire outside counsel. And after spending $800,000 and going all the way to the Virginia Supreme Court, we won our case stating that unpublished research documents are exempt from the state's Freedom of Information Act because they're still in the course of discovery and they're not the final word from the scientist. But plainly, this was motivated by skepticism about climate science and whether there is some kind of conspiracy among climate scientists that could be discovered through their e-mails. I remember a fact that Mary Sue Coleman,

Mark [Schlissel]'s predecessor as president of the University of Michigan, used to cite to me: 40 percent of the US population thinks that the earth is only four thousand years old. So I understand these issues of scientific literacy and also the ways we could get ourselves unknowingly into political disputes. One of our problems, of course, is that as academics love nuance, and much of the rest of the world focuses on sound bites. They're not compatible with each other. And so what can a young academic do, whether your field is science or the humanities or an interdisciplinary, emergent field?

Well, I think the first thing is to recognize that you are not the university, so you separate your views from the university's. Yesterday, the dean of the University of Virginia Law School told me that he's going to be testifying in Congress today, and he said, "I'm going to make the point that these views don't express the views of the University of Virginia, but no one is going to listen to that." There is some truth to that, but there is still value in saying it. The second is to separate our roles as citizens and our roles as experts. We have our first amendment right as citizens to say anything that we would like, including criticizing government. But as an expert, you restrict yourself to the field in which you do your work. So, for example, I have a nephew who is a PhD candidate at University of Wisconsin, and he studies honeybees and pollination patterns. This is a really important topic right now, with hive disease affecting a lot of American bees. So I know he's an expert when he's talking about bees and pollination and related issues. But he's been talking a lot lately about the funding of higher education in Wisconsin as well. He's speaking to that as a citizen, but he doesn't do that as an expert. And then third and finally—

and this isn't necessarily relevant to everybody—there is the need to separate the paid expert from the neutral expert. A common way of imputing the integrity of academics is to say that this work was paid for by—fill in the name of a corporation or foundation—and imply that it's discredited because of this funding source. Well, sometimes it is and sometimes it isn't, but it's important to acknowledge when you've received any kind of outside support from your work because it may color how people receive what you have to say. I think it's also useful when you are a neutral expert to be identified as such. Sometimes in the newspaper, you'll see somebody commenting on a research finding, and the newspaper will add, "Professor So-and-So did not have any relationship to the research project." Well, that's to establish that this is a neutral point of view. I think these distinctions and nuances are important, but they don't obscure the basic point that you have the right and perhaps the obligation to speak out. And I think our position as administrators is that we have the right and the obligation to protect that when faculty do.

ANDREW HOFFMAN: I'd like to push on the question of "why" now. We've heard a lot of talk about the ideal of the university and what it's supposed to be, but is there something different right now that compels this question? We can go all the way back to World War II, Vannevar Bush, and the debates that emerged over whether universities should be doing applied or basic research. Those debates continue today. Some very noted critics are saying that the university has lost the mandate of focusing on research for its own sake and is focused instead on application. Is there something different right now that makes this question more compelling, more important, that we really need to rethink what the university is?

PRESIDENT SULLIVAN: There is a fundamental critique among some that we shouldn't be doing research at all—that it's not our mission and that our mission is only teaching. And if you haven't heard that, you haven't been walking the halls of the state houses lately. Since the year 2008, there has been a questioning of the funding of higher education. Part of that has been a challenge to the research mission, and in particular, some have questioned research in the humanities and social sciences as not being a worthy thing for a university to do. So when we as administrators are defending our researchers and our faculty, one of the things we are defending is that research is something worthwhile in every discipline.

PRESIDENT HANLON: I would amplify that a little bit by expanding on the period between World War II and the early 2000s. Despite a few ups and downs, this was a period of unprecedented prosperity, economic growth, and vitality in this country. But that's changing, and with it come incredible pressures that spill over into any field where resources are needed, including higher education but many others, such as health care delivery, energy delivery, and so on. And so there are deeper and more profound tensions right now as well as complex issues that really need deep-thinking, intellectual engagements.

PRESIDENT CROW: I think the most important issue now is that most individuals have access to some form of a little supercomputer [holding up a mobile phone] that they carry in their purses, their pockets, or leave next to their beds on the nightstand. They can ask this thing any question about anything and find some kind of an answer with very little ability to determine the quality of the answer. But nonetheless, they have this ubiquitous access to information that they never had before.

The academy created these ideas, as well as the technologies and mechanisms through which this information is flowing. The University of Michigan, for example, has been a powerful force for information technology and ubiquitous information in the last few decades.

But I agree with Terry [Sullivan] and Phil [Hanlon] that there was a shift in the politics in 2008. But I think the origin of that shift is not political. I think it actually has to do with the fact that we have this ubiquity of information. You have these knowledge-producing organizations, and people don't understand the relationships or the mechanisms between them. So what we're seeing is confusion. A lot of this—what would appear to us to be ignoramuses running amok out there—is actually, in my view, confusion. There's confusion, and we haven't found the position to articulate the hierarchy of knowledge and explain the way in which knowledge evolves.

What's information? What's knowledge? What's know-how? What's not? What's this? What's that? I think that we're in an important moment, and the thing that we have to worry about now is not falling back to the period where a few people started controlling the flow of that information and manipulating the masses. We need to think seriously about this impact of technology and ubiquity of information and how we can't just say, "That's not so." What do you mean it's not so—based on what? So all things being equal, we need to make sure that people understand that there is a hierarchy to all this and get them to understand it and respect it in some way, which we have no way to do right now.

PRESIDENT SCHLISSEL: The only thing I would add is the degree of the question. I think every generation looks at itself and says, "Boy, this is the toughest time ever, and everything is under threat now, and we have it rougher than we have ever did." Well, I'm not sure that's true. I think that each generation has its challenges. Some of them are driven by changes in technology, moments in economics, moments in political discourse. This is our moment, and we have to figure out as an academy, just as our forerunners did, how to productively engage and positively influence how life plays out.

ANDREW HOFFMAN: But doesn't the role of social media have to be given its own focus? Jenny McCarthy boasts that she went to the University of Google to come up with her positions on autism and vaccines. Isn't that something that says, no, there's something different right now?

PRESIDENT SCHLISSEL: Well, certainly the ease of access of literally every human to have a worldwide platform to dispense his or her ideas is unprecedented in history, but I would imagine that in earlier eras, there were people who would speak up in a town square and just dribble out nonsense. So the effects didn't spread around the globe, but this tension among knowledge, experiment, discovery, reason, and then people's lack of respect for expertise in relation to their own opinions is not a new tension.

ANDREW HOFFMAN: President Hanlon, I have heard you talk about the idea that social media democratizes knowledge. Can you talk about that?

PRESIDENT HANLON: I think that we spend a lot of time focusing on the authors when we talk about social media, but the real challenge is to focus on the readers. I said this before: if we don't do anything else with our students, we should teach them how complex the world's issues are. We should teach them the difference between anecdote and data. We should teach them that they really have to think about things and think deeply and not just react.

PRESIDENT CROW: I just want to add one point: one of the things that has hurt us is that we've lost the control of the word or the franchise of the university. We have people out there that have no intent of doing anything that we do calling themselves "universities." We've got people running around using the word "university" to make unjustifiable profits through educational experiences that are not robust. The reason I bring this up is that I think one of the things that we need to do in this moment of time is to define what "university" means to us. In our case, we're reconceptualizing the university to be a knowledge enterprise. We produce knowledge, synthesize knowledge, store knowledge, analyze knowledge—and the three things that we produce from that process are people, ideas and concepts, and things and objects. A lot of places that call themselves universities don't do that. So we have got to find some way to recapture the term, the idea of what we actually are, because that's all being corrupted as we speak, Google University being an example.

PRESIDENT SULLIVAN: I think speed is also an important part of it. As they say, a lie makes it halfway around the world before the truth gets its shoes on. That's really true today, and something that is false or is interpreted in a false manner can be completely awash in social media before the academic community that was responsible for initiating the study even knows about it. And that's a real difficulty for us because we cannot spend all our time monitoring social media. We have other things to do. And for the people who *do* spend all their time monitoring social media, a lot of mischief can be done.

ANDREW HOFFMAN: We live in a very politically fractured time, a very divisive time. The university is perceived as a left-leaning institution, and surveys show that academics do lean left. Does that create a danger for us to step into political discourse and become political players with our work, with our research?

PRESIDENT SCHLISSEL: I think it's more of a danger that we don't create an academic community that's more intellectually and politically diverse and do so purposely. So one of the challenges I face each year is to pick graduation speakers, and it's challenging because this liberal idea is the predominant mode of thought at many universities. But I don't think we expose our

students and one another to enough thoughtful, rigorous people who represent other parts of the spectrum. I don't think we do it adequate justice. It's not going away in society, right? So unless we can create a milieu here that somewhat replicates the diversity of thought in society, it's going to be very hard for us to work through the problem. So I don't fear our faculty representing themselves and being considered liberal. I'm more concerned that we haven't created a sufficient intellectually and politically diverse community on our campus.

PRESIDENT CROW: I would just add that we have to be cautious about thinking that we live in a fractious moment. This is actually not one of the most fractious moments in American political history. We've had moments that led to the deaths of six hundred thousand Americans in a civil war. That was quite a bit more fractious. And I won't walk through all the other moments of fractiousness. I think that universities have always been places where new ideas have flowed, and both conservatives and liberals have been opposed to those new ideas repeatedly, decade after decade, generation after generation. I think the one thing that we have to do is not be political. Politics is a process that we are informing. We don't have to be political to inform politicians or political actors. If individuals want to be political, they're free to do that, but they definitively can't do that as a representative of the institution. The institution has to be, in a sense, above that when informing the process. I won't walk back through the behaviors of the American colleges and universities prior to the Civil War, but we would all be ashamed. Not of all of them but of most of them.

ANDREW HOFFMAN: Is this question different for public universities as opposed to private universities?

PRESIDENT SULLIVAN: Yes. One way it's different, of course, is simply the presence of the Freedom of Information Act. Phil [Hanlon] doesn't have to worry about that at Dartmouth. But the press can come in and demand various documents from Mark [Schlissel]'s drawer, and they can from mine, and they can from Michael [Crow]'s.

PRESIDENT CROW: I only had 167 public information requests for all my e-mails last year. [Laughter]

PRESIDENT SULLIVAN: That's different for public universities. The other thing that's different is our form of governance, which in many states is a pretty political process. The regents at the University of Michigan are elected by the people. In my own state, they're all appointed by the governor. So there is a political tone on governance that the private universities less frequently have; I won't say they never have it.

PRESIDENT HANLON: I would agree with that, but we all share a strong and appropriate interest in having open-minded discourse on our campus. So we are not immune from that legitimate interest.

PRESIDENT CROW: I was a trustee of Bowdoin College for many years, and we never spoke of politics once in any of those meetings. I was a deputy provost at Columbia University for twelve years and attended all trustee meetings for those twelve years, and we never spoke of politics there either, so it's a completely different world for the reasons that Terry [Sullivan] and the others suggest.

PRESIDENT SULLIVAN: The other thing I would say, though, is that being public universities, we're also very mindful of public service as part of our mission, and that's more exclusive in some institutions than others. But I think all of us take it seriously. And part of that service is informing a populace that lies beyond our student body. That brings back the original idea that it's important for academics to be able to get our ideas out to a broader audience.

ANDREW HOFFMAN: President Schlissel, you said that it was a tremendous honor and privilege to be a tenured professor at a major university. President Sullivan, you talked about the idea that it's the professor speaking; it's not the university speaking. Can we talk a little bit about how you see the role of the individual academic changing? To begin with, is this a question that junior faculty should be careful of getting involved in? They still have to get their tenure. Is this only a question of full professors, or is this changing the career track of all professors?

PRESIDENT SCHLISSEL: I think tenured faculty have more leeway because of the protections of tenure, but I don't necessarily believe that junior faculty members should sculpt how they want to engage with the world and what kind of impact they want to have as a scholar based on their stage of career. That falls in the category of being too careerist. You have to follow your passions. And if a part of your passion is to engage in public discourse, I think you should do that regardless of your career stage. I think one factor that we don't consider when I hear the complaint that you don't get credit for public engagement in the tenure process is that we own the tenure and promotion process; the faculties do in each of our departments. And if the department decides here in Michigan that it wants to give more weight to public engagement as part of the service or scholarly component of a faculty member's career, I think that faculty have the flexibility to define achievement in that way. We can't blame ourselves for something that we own.

ANDREW HOFFMAN: But is there a danger? Let's say a department decides engagement is part of its tenure review process. Might junior faculty members be a little crazy to follow that, because if they don't get tenure, their packets may not be as attractive in the outside market? I know that may be careerist, but we also have to be pragmatic that we do want to have lives in academia.

PRESIDENT SCHLISSEL: Yes, but those same faculty members are going to take chances by what they're writing their books on, or what research subjects they take on. I remember a junior faculty member when I was a dean at Berkeley whose goal was to determine the three-dimensional structure of something called a ribosome. This was a big deal. Everybody advised this guy, "You're nuts; if you don't get it, you're never going to get tenure." And the guy said, "I don't care; I want to understand what a ribosome looks like." So although there are pragmatic aspects

to a career, I think it's really dicey when you start telling people to do this and don't do that, because you can't ensure an outcome no matter what they do. They have to follow their passion.

PRESIDENT HANLON: Right. I would add also that there are so many great things faculty can do with their time. There is scholarship and teaching, of course, because of core missions, but then there's a professional service, there's advising, there's public service, there is any number of things they can do. And it's how they prioritize their time that really shapes their careers. I think that if junior faculty feel that engagement in public discourse is something that they value, then they should absolutely do it and put that as a priority. They still need to produce whatever they need to produce to get tenure, but beyond that, there's lots of time, and they can decide how to fill that time.

PRESIDENT SULLIVAN: I'm going to raise a warning flag about all this. For all the talk about how liberal universities are, there's nowhere we're more conservative than when it comes to tenure. I don't see the day coming when your collection of tweets is going to be accepted as a scholarly part of your tenure packet. And even if they tell you they'll accept it, they might change their minds when it comes time to vote on tenure.

PRESIDENT CROW: We have about three thousand faculty members, and they're free agents in the sense that they plot their own courses, they live by their own passions, and they decide what they want to do, but we've come up with an idea, not unique to us but one that we're implementing rather vigorously, and that is this notion of how we empower a faculty member to have greater impact. Most faculty are motivated by the desire to have recognition for their intellectual achievements. That's a fantastic motivation. So we built a unit that we're going to be growing to several hundred people, all of whom will swarm around those faculty members who want to teach the public more broadly about their research through a range of technological media in a full-immersion modality. And we're doing this through more than just the massive open online course (MOOC) platform, which lacks enough interactivity, but through a range of additional platforms.

We have one faculty member who's our best example of this, named Ariel Anbar, in our School for Earth and Space Exploration, who's emerging into this like a whole new creature. He's a Howard Hughes fellow, he's running a NASA Astrobiology Institute, and he's designing a course with funding from the Gates Foundation that could reach a million students by the time it's done. It will teach fundamental skills necessary for freshmen-level college understanding of science and will be taught through a completely different modality of teaching through exploration. What that means is that he becomes an unbelievably empowered, individually driven, passion-driven faculty member who will conduct research, advance scholarship, and secure his academic position through his scholarship but also become this projected force by connecting to the public in a different way. We think there's a huge opportunity for that kind of model to help break down the barrier between universities and those not able to physically be with us. For us, it's a big deal.

ANDREW HOFFMAN: Does the kind of change we are discussing require change across the institution of academia, or can one university or one school within a university or one department within a school do this on its own?

PRESIDENT CROW: I go back to my idea of a free agent. All our schools, all our individual faculty, are free agents. So there's no mechanism to say that we're all going to go this way. Are you kidding me? We can't even get everybody to show up to a meeting. We look at what percentage opened the e-mail that we sent—8 percent! Chances are that we're not going to get everybody to go together. So one has to create these opportunities for individual innovations, school innovations, center innovations. We talked ear-

lier, Mark [Schlissel], about individual universities innovating in different ways—differentiation. So it's all about differentiation and enabling innovation.

ANDREW HOFFMAN: When this conversation started, it sounded to me like there was a collective problem. Can we expect individual free agents to fix or address the problem, or does it have to be addressed collectively? I hate to be pushing on this, but I think it's important.

PRESIDENT SCHLISSEL: I think it is a leadership thing and leadership at many different levels. But someone in the president's position or a dean or chair's position can motivate behavior by celebrating individuals and their successes. Our communications people capture every day the comments that hit the national media from our faculty, and that's a celebration of their success. If somebody appears in a prominent position that's newsworthy, we push that out there. So I think that's one way the leadership can signal this is something we want our faculty to do. But as I mentioned in my earlier comments, this isn't a mandate that all three thousand instructional faculty, and nonclinical instructional faculty in Michigan, and everybody have to do. It's just a component of an academic career that we respect.

PRESIDENT CROW: One of the courses that I taught at Columbia was for all students who were receiving National Institutes for Health (NIH) fellowships or NIH support to teach the public duty of the publicly funded scientist. And I could tell by the resistance of the students to taking the course that they hated it. The question that was asked was, "Who are you to tell me what my public duty is?" This goes to the root of your question. Our culture is not fully preparing our academics for engagement in the complex society in which we rest. So that's something that we're going to have to do, and that's a responsibility that leaders of institutions are going to have to take on and move in a different way. And we've been working on that in my institution's case, but I remember from the years that I've taught that course at Columbia that it was hard, because people say, "Get out of my face and leave me alone; I'm going to do whatever I want to do, and the rest of you can just drop dead." That was kind of the attitude of these graduate students. These were NIH-supported graduate students who had to take this course as a function of their funding.

PRESIDENT HANLON: I would also remember that our promotion processes, our funding processes, are designed to ensure that faculty will continue to do exactly the kind of work that allows them to speak to public issues. It actually doesn't help to have someone speaking to public issues whose work is not deep and valued. So that's exactly what our tenure processes are designed to ensure.

ANDREW HOFFMAN: As we start to think about the role of the tenured professor or the full professor changing in these times, becoming more of public intellectual, can you imagine what that change in role might look like? I remember a funny quip by one of my colleagues. We were walking through campus, and he said, you know, "One of the problems I see around me in academia is we have too many senior professors thinking like junior professors." They are still chasing those individual pieces of knowledge and not bringing them together for the benefit of society. Can you envision what we might do not to try to recreate one design for the full professor but to broaden the perspective of what it means? Can you give some thought to what that range of activities or roles or personas might look like?

PRESIDENT SULLIVAN: One thing I would say about full professors is that they are much more actively engaged typically in peer review. That is a very important part of quality assurance. And one of the disturbing things to me in the last couple of years has been the attack on peer review. But most full professors I know spend lots of time assessing and evaluating their peers because they're editors of journals, they're reviewing manuscripts, they're writing letters of recommendation for their students or for colleagues, or they're just spending a lot of time in what I call "assessment." It's an important and underappreciated part of the professorial role.

PRESIDENT HANLON: I think it is really interesting when faculty are able to come in contact with practitioners. We all have mechanisms on all our campuses to bring grant practitioners to campus, and I think they really liven the environment.

PRESIDENT CROW: I have served on one of the National Science Foundation and National Academies panels mentioned in the introductory comments. Now imagine if we could build identities for each and every one of our faculty members that express their passions. Why are they doing this, whether they're English literature professors, or biologists, or whatever? What is the

"why"? And we find some way to help them if they can't express that on their own. And then beyond that, we help them define an identity and articulate the ideas that they're pursuing, their discourse with other people. We're working on this—finding ways to translate some of the things that they're working on that might not be easily understandable by others. This is an expensive and time-consuming process that you wouldn't want to burden the faculty members with themselves. We're starting to create positions of knowledge curators and educational technology specialists who will be working with our faculty to project their identities and build translation capabilities around them. All their courses, all their interactive learning environments, everything that they're doing, all the digital ways that we have to link things together, and with that, a full professor in this particular world becomes like a super faculty member. I don't know what to call it, but there's got to be a way to elevate this person who has achieved national or international status as a full professor, which took decades to achieve, and he or she needs to be visible to the public. Scholars don't have the kind of identity in the United States that they have in China and other places, and there are reasons for that that need to be addressed. And so we're talking about how you build the identity of and interactive engagement with the faculty member, which can be then greatly enhanced by finding a way to project and translate that identity.

PRESIDENT SCHLISSEL: There are two other trends in the academy that I've noticed that are increasing in recent years. One is this mode of education called engaged learning; that's a set of circumstances that is going to put more and more faculty outside the academy working with their students on real-world problems and lead them to think of themselves more as contributors beyond the edge of the campus. The other is the enormous and growing popularity of entrepreneurship programs on campus: social entrepreneurship and business entrepreneurship. That's also an externally focused activity driven by the needs and demands of our students, but I think the faculty will end up following that and, perhaps with the generational change, will develop more of an outward focus driven by student interest.

ANDREW HOFFMAN: Do you see any dangers to this kind of activity? Is there a line someone can cross? Is there a point at which they are no longer objective academics; they're subjective pundits. Paul Krugman, for example, is a rigorous thinker who has devoted his career to editorials and public positions. Are there activities that would start to raise some red flags in your book of going too far in this thinking?

PRESIDENT SULLIVAN: So my first political science instructor was George Will, but today, George Will would not describe himself in the same way. We have to allow that to happen—allow people to pursue their careers. That happens to academics as well. And I don't think you want to limit them in doing it. If they wish to stay affiliated with the university now, there are certain minimal things we're going to continue to ask them to do. At my university, one of those is engagement with students. That's simply part of the full package at the University of Virginia. But yes, I think there's room for people's careers to change and go in different directions and for people to change disciplines. Interdisciplinary programs get developed because people are willing to broach the boundary of their discipline with another discipline. If we didn't have people brave enough to do that, there are lots of fields that would not exist in the current university.

PRESIDENT SCHLISSEL: So how do you define a pundit for the purpose of this question? Writing an op-ed every once in a while is OK. If you're an expert and you have this platform that lets you reach thought leaders all around the world and you do it three times a week, is that all of a sudden punditry?

ANDREW HOFFMAN: That's a great question. We all know that in our culture if people drift away from doing research and if their resumes become filled with nothing but editorials, we would look at them askance. And if they become associated with a particular political position that is not necessarily grounded in research, then they are no longer part of the community of what we consider to be legitimate academics. I'm pushing the boundaries here because I think we're stepping into new territory.

PRESIDENT CROW: Well, it's not so new. Carl Sagan was a fantastically successful planetary scientist at Cornell University and was, among the planetary scientists, probably the best translator both through his *Cosmos* show and through his novels like *Contact* and other things that he did, and he reached tens of millions of people. If you talked to planetary scientists who ridiculed him for taking on the role, he was right and they were wrong. It's as simple as that.

ANDREW HOFFMAN: Do you think that culture still exists?

PRESIDENT CROW: Certainly, it still exists. It's based on many human emotions, but I think the base may be jealousy. The notion that somehow a Carl Sagan can be a successful scientist and then, after having demonstrated his ability to be a successful scientist—as successful as any other—can go out and be unbelievably creative in other ways while still teaching graduate students and students at Cornell is important. He's not a lesser person for emerging as a public intellectual. We only have a few hundred of those in the United States. Paul Krugman is one; George Will is one. They each have a different view of the world, but they're each of that class. Unfortunately, not enough of them are coming from the academy in my view. And so if one can emerge from the academy and fulfill that kind of role while still teaching and contributing to the university and so forth, then hallelujah, because it's a way to get discourse to the higher level.

PRESIDENT HANLON: I believe that we are operating under a premise in this conversation that when we talk about engagement with publications, we're talking about critical thinking and analysis rather than creating solutions for the world's issues. That's another very important thing the academy does. And we're having this interesting debate on our campus right now as we're creating an entity to find solutions for health care delivery. We have an existing entity that has conducted academic analysis of health care delivery, and now we are asking if those two should be separate or if they could be merged together; would that sort of engagement poison the integrity of it?

ANDREW HOFFMAN: President Crow, you said that bias still exists and that Carl Sagan was not respected. What are the formal and informal obstacles to changing the university to encourage more of these kinds of people to emerge? If you could break down the obstacles on your campus, what would they be?

PRESIDENT CROW: We allow people to say things in academia that are unbelievable. We allow people to attack the Carl Sagans of the world. And everybody else that thinks that Carl Sagan is doing the right thing, but they don't really say anything. It's the weirdest thing I've ever seen. They're just kind of quiet. And so, to me, we have to find a way for university leadership to protect and defend the translators who emerge from among us and to encourage and empower them—help them get out and perform this translation function. There are not very many people who can do that, and they're sorely needed, but they're suppressed in our own environment by people who are so very interested in maintaining this status quo that they keep the Carl Sagans of the world from emerging. Everybody else has to tell *those* people to just be quiet.

PRESIDENT HANLON: I would agree that we really need more speaking out among our faculty. Also I think what Mark [Schlissel] said earlier was really correct in my experience; our faculty are free agents. They're entrepreneurs, and what we can do most effectively is to celebrate the pioneers and make sure they have everything they need, and when they do great stuff, just shadow them thereafter.

PRESIDENT SCHLISSEL: We maintain databases of people of expertise, and when journalists come to us, we'll direct them toward the faculty colleague who wants to be a spokesperson in an area. We can provide media training for people and give them the skills to do what's part of their passion more effectively. And again, as I said, we can celebrate their successes.

PRESIDENT SULLIVAN: But the obstacle is in each department. That's where a lot of fundamental rewards get distributed. And I'm not just speaking of money, although money is one of those rewards. Departments have their own cultures and customs, and as human beings, they're also subject to envy and other such negative emotions. It's hard to rescue your Carl Sagans from those departmental situations. And sometimes it's just a reality that while you've got someone who is out being famous, there's work that needs to get done, and that person is not lifting that share of the load. Thus it can really be boiled down to simple issues such as that.

ANDREW HOFFMAN: We have people lining up for questions, so let's begin.

QUESTION 1, DEBRA ROWE (US PARTNERSHIP FOR EDUCATION FOR SUSTAINABLE DEVELOPMENT): We have found that it doesn't work to point to the innovators because all the obedient middles would go, "Well, that's them." So if we're really going to build more public intellectuals and create professors who can do community engagement on real-world problem solving with quality, you can't count on the departments to make these tenure guideline changes alone. You guys have power to create systemic change. What changes do we need in how we teach our PhD students so that when they do community engagement, they actually know how to do it? And how do we change this tenure system that keeps your obedient middles doing stuff that's less than optimal?

PRESIDENT SCHLISSEL: I'd say the scope of the problem is too huge to focus on just the tenure piece of it. But university presidents are less powerful than you think. We don't get to define what the standards are. If I put out a memo that said, "I'd like you departments to approach things in this way," it might get very few clicks. I think the senior leadership has influence in directing resources, being a positive reinforcer of the kind of behaviors that are occurring and celebrating success, and building infrastructure around people and activities that you want to support. I'm hopeful that concepts of tenure will evolve, but I'm not seeing great examples.

PRESIDENT CROW: This goes to something Mark [Schlissel] and I were talking about earlier this morning: we really need to be careful about assuming that all these things that we're calling universities are the same. They're not all the same. They're actually different. I'll just use Michigan and Arizona State University as examples. So let's pretend that Michigan is a classic class M planet. It's a certain type of planet. It's got a certain kind of atmosphere, it works in certain ways, and it has cultures and microcultures that are very similar to the class N planet that I'm on, but our planets are different. It just so happens in our particular planet that we decided the class M planets would make curiosity-driven research the core fundamental value driving the overall design of the institution, and we said, "That's a good value, but let's add use-inspired research to that as the core intellectual value." So on the N planet, drawing from the value system of the M planet, it's slightly different. One of the things that we do is we overgeneralize universities as being more similar than they actually are. We need to start saying, well, no, we have these ten types of universities. They're working in these ten types of arenas. There's a core value system underlying all of them, which is free and open discourse—all the things that came from the great Greek academies. Those are still a part of what we all do, but we're going to operate differently. As a result, you would have differentiated models for tenure and differentiated markets for faculty to work. I might not want to work at an N-class planet. I might want to work at an M-class planet. And then this array of universities will, in the long run, help provide us with an opportunity to have an even more diverse higher education community—one more likely to be able to handle the 450 million people that we're going to have, to educate them at higher levels, and to solve more problems down the road. And so tenure is a word that will have related and similar but different meanings across all these institutions.

ANDREW HOFFMAN: That begs the question of the rankings and what they do to normalize the idea that there's only one kind of planet—one measure of quality.

PRESIDENT CROW: None of those rankings were developed by us, by the academy itself. They're all developed by profit-seeking magazines attempting to manipulate the behavior of parents sending their kids to college.

PRESIDENT HANLON: You asked the question about how we prepare our graduate students for engagement and public discourse. I would point out that we're really not the best people to prepare them, because we don't know how to do that ourselves. And so there are initiatives that do that quite well. The op-ed project is one; Alan Alda's institute at Stony Brook is a really interesting place. It's all about how you communicate science. So, in fact, there are experts in doing that. They're alive and operating within the academy. I'm sure there are others; those are just two I know about, but we as faculty are probably not the best people to do that.

QUESTION 2, ANDREW SCHWARTZ (DOCTORAL STUDENT, UNIVERSITY OF MICHIGAN): Do you think that this effort to engage the public or inform the public will be successful via direct interaction between the academy and the public? Or do you think that the mainstream media needs to fulfill this role and bridge the gap? And if so, could you please comment on the role that corporate media has played in creating and enabling the divide between the academy and society more broadly?

PRESIDENT SCHLISSEL: The one discouraging thing for me about the mainstream media is the depth of coverage. I'm a chronic *New York Times* reader. It's the first thing I do every morning. I go down to the kitchen, get the newspaper, and read it before I come to work. Anytime I read an article about which I have expert level knowledge, I realize it's not quite right.

PRESIDENT CROW: That's every time, right?

PRESIDENT SCHLISSEL: Every single time. But sometimes it's better than others. It's challenging, and I think about how hard it is to be a journalist and write one day about immunology and the next day about microbiology, even if you're a science journalist. So I don't think we can really rely on the media to drive this. I think we have to be proactive, and those of us who care will have to make the news.

PRESIDENT CROW: I want to add that we have to up our game within the universities and the expressions of what we do so as to take the more responsible elements of corporate media and help them up their game. There will be the irresponsible journalists who only care about their own outcomes; they don't care about the veracity of what they do. So forget those people, because there's not much we can do with them; they're motivated by other things. But that's not everybody. If we up our game, they'll up their game, and so that's basically the approach I think we need to take.

PRESIDENT SCHLISSEL: The serious journalists want to get it right. I'm not impugning their ethics or their characters. It's just hard to get it right if you're an outsider.

PRESIDENT HANLON: They're often taking something very technical that we offer them and trying to translate it into something the public can digest. So they've got a tough job. I'm also a *New York Times* reader every morning. I also read the *Wall Street Journal*; I put them side by side. It's interesting to read the same story through each lens. And they take on some really difficult challenges in trying to make complex issues understandable.

ANDREW SCHWARTZ: Can I ask a follow-up? Do you think that the fact that these corporate media outlets such as *New York Times* are for-profit institutions means that they are not as unbiased as we claim we are in the academy?

PRESIDENT SCHLISSEL: Well, I think they're trying to attract readers, but I think the serious media does have serious ethical standards, and they really are trying to get it right. But they're also trying to attract eyeballs. They're going to choose topics to write about that they think will interest the public. So I guess the way we can interface with that is by making what we think is important interesting to the public.

PRESIDENT SULLIVAN: But I do think it's an issue that there are shrinking numbers of journalists in all those outlets, so you have fewer and fewer people in the newsroom every day trying to cover every possible subject.

PRESIDENT SCHLISSEL: Yes.

QUESTION 3, MATTHEW WOZNIAK (DOCTORAL STUDENT, UNIVERSITY OF MICHIGAN): I'd like to touch on the question of nuances versus sound bites. Look at the venues that put out sound bites, like Twitter or Facebook or other social media; that's a very efficient way of getting ideas and facts out to the public, and it's really what most people are looking at as their source of information. And as Dr. Crow mentioned, it's like you wake up in the morning and check Facebook; you just scroll through. But how do you quality-check this information? All our academic papers go up in these journals at $40 a pop, and I can't imagine it's very easy for the average person to go in and check the information. Are they supposed to e-mail out to the people that are responsible for the information or so on? So I have a couple questions that relate to that. Can Twitter, Facebook, or any sources like that ever have authority? Could that be the quality itself? Could that institution be of high quality? And second, how can we bridge the gap between that and our nuanced information in journals and articles? How can we find a middle ground between that and sound bites?

PRESIDENT SULLIVAN: The difficulty with Twitter or Facebook being accepted as credible is that you don't have a quality apparatus, something like peer review, currently available for that. Could that be developed? Maybe it's possible. I don't know. On the other hand, when you do have peer review, it's expensive, and you've got to pay for that apparatus. So you're right—lots of ordinary readers don't get access to the journals because even if they go to their public library, the library doesn't have it. If they go to one of our university libraries, they may not have access because of copyright restrictions, and all those restrictions in turn are there to protect the journal's ability to keep putting the journal out. So there is indeed a big gap between sound bite and nuance. And I think one thing that some authors do, which is helpful, is provide an e-mail address or some other way that people could get additional information. Some media outlets do that routinely. Frequently—on National Public Radio, for example—you'll get enough information about the scientist whose work is presented that you could actually contact that person. But I don't think we've got the issue of the gap figured out yet, and maybe there's some new interstitial medium we don't know about yet, or that hasn't been invented yet, that will help us do that.

PRESIDENT SCHLISSEL: I think one of the interesting and underappreciated aspects of social media is that it really can be an accurate gauge of what people are thinking, the users of social media. It's not a gauge of what's true or false or misleading or correct. Certainly, you could do analytics on the massive amount of information that Twitter and Facebook are holding on to, and God knows what they're doing with it now, and it would be a great gauge of public thought. And I just wanted to say this about the survey result you mentioned, Andy, in your introduction about the 40 percent of respondents that said that they never thought they'd use Twitter in their whole lives and they would die if they did: I was in that group, and you know, I'm still standing, but it's just a terrible medium.

PRESIDENT HANLON: The credible mainstream media has actually played the role you just asked about. You could argue whether they play it well or not, or whether we need a different kind of mechanism, but I think that's exactly the kind of role they're trying to play.

QUESTION 4, ARTHUR LUPIA (UNIVERSITY OF MICHIGAN): Each of you in your presidencies is offering provocative and compelling visions of the future of higher education, and your success is critical to your communities and to the nation. But we live in an increasingly competitive communication environment where the information we're trying to provide is fighting with all the other sources you've mentioned. So the question I want to ask is, suppose for a moment that you weren't a university president—suppose you were university dictator, and you either had the ability to add a program or asset that would help you adapt or had the ability to change or jettison a legacy institution that you think would help your university provide more information of more value to more people. What would you do?

PRESIDENT CROW: With the support of our faculty, we've eliminated eighty-three academic units in

the last few years and restructured, at the design of the faculty, many dozens of new configurations. That has been an empowering process 85 to 90 percent of the time. That's a very high percentage. As for the others, that's a mess, so it doesn't always work. And so, if I had an inordinate temporary potentate-type influence for just a day, I would empower our faculty and basically say to them, please do not just accept the standard-issue social construct that you know as your department or your school. What is it that you really think we should be doing? What is it that you really think we should be having as our trajectory? Free yourself from this conservatism that exists out there. You may come back and say it's exactly the way we want it to be. But it will be because you decided it as opposed to you inheriting it and barely understanding it.

PRESIDENT HANLON: I think that we have always provided our students with two qualitatively different things. One is knowledge about the world—just the facts of the world and intellectual frameworks we create so those facts make sense to us. On the other hand, we give them the skills to be successful in the world—communication skills, a creative mind, critical thinking skills, numeracy, the ability to engage the arts and humanities, and so on. And we have forever developed mechanisms to test knowledge acquisition, because it's easy to test. We have never known how to test skills development, so if I could do one thing, it would be to jettison the current modes of evaluating student performance and develop modes that test their development of skills. And skills development is one thing that is really difficult to deliver online.

PRESIDENT SCHLISSEL: I'm going to listen to smart guys like that and go back to my office and do what they said.

PRESIDENT CROW: I agree with Phil [Hanlon], too. His ideas are better than what I thought of.

PRESIDENT SCHLISSEL: Those are really bold, spectacular ideas that can come from this mythical power that certainly won't exist during the time I'm president here. To get to the practical, the real sweet spot is learning how to morph the structures and practices we have now and promote the management to change to get to a better place where we can capture the strength of disciplines but not be bound by them. We need to come to realize that we carry access to the world's information in our pockets, so we don't need to teach students too many facts. We need to teach them how to think and analyze and how to look for facts. So going from where we are now in the direction of the places my colleagues suggest is, I think, actually achievable.

PRESIDENT SULLIVAN: I think these are all really interesting ideas. If I could do just one thing, I would get rid of the semester, because I think it is an artificial constraint on the way that we package the information that we want students to have. Some subjects can be well taught in a couple of weeks, and some take a whole year, but we try to shoehorn everything into the same uniform fifteen-week semester. And we do it because it's convenient, and I understand that. But I think there are ways that we could reconfigure a student's educational trajectory and perhaps do it in such a way that lets him or her leave in three years rather than four. There's nothing magic about four, and some students are more than ready to enter the next phase of life after three years. But we constrain ourselves not only in terms of the space of departments but also in terms of the time that we set for teaching courses.

PRESIDENT CROW: We did that three years ago, and it's very interesting. We can talk about that in terms of the kinds of very positive results but lots of stresses also.

QUESTION 5, RYAN MEYER (CALIFORNIA OCEAN SCIENCE TRUST): One thing I'd like to caution against is the savior mentality because I think that could be quite self-defeating, whether or not we think there are problems with public and political discourse. And remember that engagement is going to have arrows going both directions. So if we just think we need to be shouting more effectively at the public, we're not going to get very far. And so in that light, I'd be interested in how you see universities and academia benefiting from engagement in public and political discourse. I think the idea that we have to do it because it's our responsibility is a very preservationist idea. I think I agree with it, but whether it's pedagogy, the framing of research agendas, or the constitution of new centers, there are so many potential ways that listening and learning from neighborhoods around the university, all the way up to global dynamics, can really improve universities.

PRESIDENT SCHLISSEL: I think that's a point enormously well taken. Interestingly, I think one of the advantages of being a public institution is that we all have public forms of governance. Although we might wring our hands and bristle from time to time, that governance really does tell us what the public thinks, what the public cares about, and what the public wants us to do, and I think that's an important directionality of information as well. So I think you made a great point.

PRESIDENT CROW: At Arizona State University, we developed a series of eight design aspirations, one of which is that our place is the single most important part of our identity. And if we're not reflective of the place, then we will have failed. We drew these design aspirations from the writings of a whole range of people, but most notably Frank Rhodes, who was president at Cornell for a number of years and wrote a book called *Creating the Future,* and also Jim Duderstadt, who wrote a book called *A University for the 21st Century.* The second of the eight is what we call "social embeddedness," which is the two-way highway. This is not suggesting that every university has to do this, but it's suggesting that some universities need to move into this modality. These have been very difficult things for us to implement over the last ten-plus years. But nonetheless, they have altered the behavior, psychology, and culture of our faculty in positive and creative ways. As you say, the arrows are moving in both directions.

QUESTION 6, AMY SCHALET (UNIVERSITY OF MASSACHUSETTS, AMHERST): It's been mentioned a few times that the skills to do public and political engagement are not ones we learn at the university. And it was mentioned also that we're not really the ones to teach those skills. And at the Public Engagement Project at UMass Amherst, we take a slightly different approach. We actually think that faculty—we're a faculty-driven initiative—who have done public engagement are in a good position to understand the anxieties of other people with PhDs and the problems of translating knowledge and the dangers that come up. So it's a slightly different approach, and one of the points we often make is that public engagement does have to actually be a two-way relationship for it to work. So I just want to throw it into the mix that there's something that faculty can offer other faculty. I also wanted to quickly ask a question: if you'd be willing to develop that point that if we are empowered within the university to redefine tenure and we can in fact do that to reward engagement, what are the tensions from senior administrators all the way down to faculty about the potential loss of status if that were to happen?

PRESIDENT HANLON: I was the one who suggested that faculty aren't in the best position to teach students and others to engage. And in part, it is because I think it's harder than it appears. I was recently on a network TV show and was asked an incredibly complex question and told I had a minute and a half to answer. Unless you're prepared for that, it's something that's not that easy. It's a lot harder than it appears, and there is some actual expertise that goes with it. On the second question, the one thing I worry about is that we have to remember the core reason for the tenure process, and it really is to be totally convinced that the person's productivity and scholarly work will continue. That's really the thing we're after before we award a lifetime contract, which is an incredible privilege. So I don't really care what the elements are or how we engineer it, but I do care that we ensure continued productivity in scholarship and teaching out of the process.

PRESIDENT CROW: I view tenure similarly but slightly differently. It does have a property right and is based on a contract, but its purpose in my view is a lifetime license to advance your academic agenda, your theory production, and your creativity without encumbrance from those who own the theories that you are replacing. So in the United States at a number of prominent institutions, there's a history of individuals who were attacking the theories or the assumptions of others being ridiculed by their faculty, colleagues, or industrial interests around the institutions and ultimately fired. And so the notion of tenure is a license for your expression and your creativity to be unencumbered. It's not a license to not do work; it's not a license to hide. So there are limits to all this, but this notion of somehow broadening what faculty members do to project their academic identity beyond just a narrow band, that's a school-by-school and discipline-by-discipline kind of thing within certain kinds of parameters. I think there's lots of room for the innovation, renovation, and improvement of the idea, scope, and implementation of tenure. But it's going to be highly variable within schools and between schools.

ANDREW HOFFMAN: It's time to bring this session to a close. I'd like to thank you for coming here. I think your presence has signaled the importance and the urgency of the questions we're asking, and I think the conversation we just had will lay the foundation for the panels and the discussions that will follow. So thank you very much. [Applause]

6 DELIVERING ON SCIENCE'S SOCIAL CONTRACT

Jane Lubchenco

ANDREW MAYNARD: Good evening, and welcome to this evening's keynote. It gives me very great pleasure to welcome the Honorable Jane Lubchenco here tonight. Dr. Lubchenco is, in very many ways, the personification of this meeting's theme. She's an internationally respected academic, she was a political appointee under President Obama, and she has long championed public discourse around science. Dr. Lubchenco is, by training, a marine ecologist and environmental scientist. She currently holds the title of Distinguished University Professor and Advisor in Marine Studies at Oregon State University. Her academic publication list is equally distinguished. She is one of the most cited ecologists in the world, and eight of her publications are recognized as science citation classics. Her academic CV is, to say the least, weighty. Her list of achievements, appointments, and accolades puts most of us to shame. Certainly when I was reading it, I felt a little more than inadequate.

By any metric, Dr. Lubchenco is a highly active and highly accomplished scientist and academic, but she's far more than this. In 2008, then president-elect Barack Obama nominated her as part of his science dream team. In 2009, she was confirmed by the Senate as administrator of NOAA, the National Oceanic and Atmospheric Administration. Under her leadership, NOAA made advances in a number of areas, including restoring fisheries to sustainability and profitability, restoring oceans and coasts to a healthy state, advancing climate science, and providing information on climate change understanding and preparedness. It's probably an understatement to say that in her term as NOAA administrator, Dr. Lubchenco engaged in her fair share of political discourse. And as she did so, she emerged as a scientist who could hold her own on the political stage. So by my reckoning, that takes two of the three selection criteria for this evening's keynote talk: the academic one and the political one.

But how about the public discourse one? Not surprisingly, this is also an area where Dr. Lubchenco shines. Between 1997 and 1998, she served as president of the American Association for the Advancement of Science. Her presidential address was titled, very importantly for tonight, "Entering the Century of the Environment: A New Social Contract with Science." The address reflected a deep realization of the importance of public discourse between scientists and other academics and citizens. It presented then—and in many ways, it still does—a radical vision of the responsibility academics have to be a part of the society that they work in and that they serve. And while Dr. Lubchenco's focus was on the environment, it's also fair to say that her idea of the environment is very broad, encompassing health, societal, and economic, as well as ecological, dimensions. This passion for public discourse goes deep. Dr. Lubchenco was cofounder of the Leopold Leadership Program, which supports professional training and engagement with leaders in the public and private sectors. She also cofounded COMPASS, an organization dedicated to helping scientists connect with others and share their knowledge. And as if that wasn't sufficient, she cofounded Climate Central, a nonprofit news organization that analyzes and reports on climate science.

It is no surprise, given her many accomplishments, that earlier this year, Dr. Lubchenco was awarded the prestigious Tyler Prize for Environmental Achievement in recognition of a career dedicated to performing policy with sound science and engaging with local communities. So when it comes to the nexus among academia, politics, and the public, Dr. Lubchenco is a passionate and knowledgeable expert with a unique insight into what it takes to ensure academic studies are intimately connected with the society that supports them. And so without further ado, please join me in welcoming the Honorable Dr. Jane Lubchenco. [Applause]

JANE LUBCHENCO: Thank you, Andrew. My compliments to you, Andy Hoffman, and the team of folks who have conceived and organized this discourse. Engaging diverse perspectives and experiences on these topics is critically important. I look forward to the outcome of your deliberations.

As an environmental scientist, I think about the questions that you have been discussing today in light of my own experiences in the world of science, engagement, management, policy, and public understanding. My remarks therefore will focus on science, but I believe that they are equally applicable for academic scholarship more generally. So if I say "science," you should feel free to hear "academic scholarship" in my remarks. I plan to draw liberally on my experiences in academia and in government, and I'll take the liberty of sharing a few stories with you along the say. I will focus initially on the "why" (Why academics should be more engaged with society); then touch on the "when" (When should they do so?), the "who" (Everyone? Just some academics?), and the "how" (How to engage effectively); and finally end with some reflections on some of the choices that exist for academics, the enabling conditions for success, and how to avoid the pitfalls.

I'll begin with a framing question for you: "What is the role of science in society?" Put differently, if you were meeting with a member of Congress and you were trying to convince him or her about the importance of funding science, what would you highlight? Or if you were a member of Congress, what would you tell your colleagues about the reasons to fund science? You probably each have your own ideas. Most people, in my experience, will focus on one of five different benefits that science provides:

1. *Science as an engine of economic growth.* That has played well in Congress over the years.
2. *Science to conquer disease and improve human health.* This benefit also clearly resonates with members of Congress: witness NIH's budget over the last few decades.
3. *Science to enable national security.* There was a big bump in investment in science post-9/11.
4. *Science to improve our lives through technology.* Smartphones are a great example.
5. *Science to enhance national competitiveness and set us apart from other nations.* Elected representatives around the world often tout this rationale. Being able to brag about the number of Nobel Prizes a country has or to win the race to the moon are examples.

I believe there are two other less frequently articulated but important roles for science:

6. Science simply to satisfy our own innate curiosity about how the world works.
7. Science to inform our own understanding of a variety of issues.

This notion of "science to inform" is one many academics readily identify but is not often mentioned by others. It is worth a deeper look. I would single out five different ways in which knowledge can benefit understanding. Scientific knowledge can inform an understanding of the following:

1. How something works—how your body works, how an ecosystem functions, or how the economy works—that is, a focus on mechanisms, on processes.
2. How that thing—let's say the world—is changing, for example, as a result of climate change. This element requires a temporal component—for example, the result of monitoring through time.
3. Using the knowledge about how it works and is changing, what are the likely future states under a business-as-usual situation? This is simply a projection of the current trajectory, informed by an understanding of dynamics.
4. Are there different possible futures, and which interventions would most likely result in which outcomes? For example, would a particular antibiotic likely cure the infection you have? Or what would be the likely impact on climate change of different emission reduction scenarios?
5. What solutions exist or could be invented to address important problems? New medicines, new solar technology, new policy, and management approaches are all examples.

The first two elements of "science to inform" focus on the past and present. The last three look ahead to the future, a future with and without interventions. Scientific knowledge can assist decision making in all five.

The assumption I am making is that decisions that are informed by a scientific understanding are going to be better decisions. The information that I just described, for example, would assist individuals and societies in understanding the trade-offs in making decisions about different possible options, for example, with respect to climate change. Obviously, the knowledge in any of these arenas is not perfect, and care must be taken to communicate degrees of certainty and uncertainty.

I want to be very clear here. I'm not suggesting a simplistic "deficit model" in which an audience is simply an empty vessel that needs filling up with scientific knowledge, and then that audience will do whatever the filler-upper would want them to do. Nor am I talking about science dictating any particular outcome. The concept of "science to inform, not dictate" explicitly acknowledges that there are multiple factors that will likely affect decisions made by an individual or an institution—factors such as politics, economics, values, expediency, or peer pressure, for example. My point is that science should also be at the table, not just those other factors.

Unfortunately, all too often, scientific knowledge is not at the table, and it's important to ask why. In my experience, scientific information is often not taken into account because the information is not readily available, or it's not understandable, or it's not seen as being relevant or useful, or it's not seen as being credible to the person making the decision. Oftentimes, it's a combination of many or all of those.

Scientists bear responsibility for all of these failures, to varying degrees. And we can be proactive in addressing the reasons why scientific information is often not available, understandable, useable, or credible. For example, in my experience, many, many people, including many politicians, simply assume they won't understand what a scientist is saying. "It's too technical!" "I don't understand all those big words!" "Scientists caveat everything so much; I guess they don't aren't confident about anything." These are statements I've heard multiple times. I think this is highly unfortunate. I'm reminded of an experience I had during my tenure at NOAA.

We were in the middle of dealing with the Deepwater Horizon oil spill disaster. About a month into the spill, the president asked the vice president to travel to the Gulf and meet with fishermen to listen to their concerns and talk about what we knew about oil and seafood and what the federal government was doing to ameliorate the threat. The VP indicated he was happy to go to the Gulf but said he needed somebody with him who knew about fisheries and what was happening to the oil in the Gulf. I had not worked with the VP before, but I was asked to accompany him to the Gulf. So I flew on Air Force Two to the Gulf with him and began to brief him on the plane. I described what we knew about oil, fisheries, and the Gulf. I told him that oil is pretty nasty stuff because it contains toxins, some of which cause cancer. But most fish can metabolize those toxins, so after a while, their muscles are no longer contaminated. I described how other kinds of seafood, such as crabs or shrimp, can also metabolize the toxins, but they do so more slowly, and how oysters and clams can't metabolize the toxins at all, so once they're contaminated, they're always contaminated. I explained that NOAA was closing federal waters to fishing in areas where oil was present or would be present in the next twenty-four, forty-eight, or seventy-two hours based on our knowledge of where the oil was and our models showing where it would go, and so on. Partway through this explanation, the vice president said, "Hey, wait a minute. I thought you were a scientist." And I said (more than a little apprehensively), "I am." Then he said, "But . . . I just understood everything you told me!" Much relieved, I continued to brief him and answer his questions, while also thinking, "Oh, my goodness. What a condemnation his statement was of the hundreds of scientists who have briefed this distinguished politician over many, many years. He thinks he can't understand us." Unfortunately, he's not alone. Most people aren't quite as forthcoming as the VP in articulating impressions of scientists, but I have heard far too many similar assessments.

One of my pleas to other scientists is to learn to become what I call "bilingual." I think scientists need to be able to speak the language of science with all of its jargon, all of its nuances, all of its caveats, but we also need to be able to speak the language of laypeople—to be able to translate very complicated things into something that's understandable and do so in a way that's credible.

In fact, despite the open antipathy toward science that does exist in some quarters, I've found a pervasive and real hunger for credible information among decision makers, ranging from policy makers to business and civic leaders to ordinary citizens. I am also well aware of the wealth of information that's not being incorporated into understanding and decisions. We thus have a golden opportunity, should we choose to engage.

Far too often, academics have assumed that it is sufficient to share the results of their discoveries in the peer-reviewed literature, in technical journals, and at scientific conferences. They think it's the job of an academic to discover new knowledge and to publish it. Period. I think there's often a vague sense that it's somebody else's job to translate this knowledge for the general public, business leaders, and policy and management decision makers. Perhaps there are knowledge-translation elves that magically appear at night and translate knowledge from academic lingo in scholarly journals to plain language in readily accessible places. Sounds pretty nice, actually! In fact, there are some translators that do just that—science journalists, for example—but they are becoming fewer and fewer. And even in the heyday of science journalism, they were insufficient to do all the translation that was needed. Moreover, engagement in the way that I think about it is more than just translation—but park that thought for now, and let's come back to it. My point here is simply that the need for translation is far greater than the current ability of translators to deliver it.

Moreover, in my view, the scholars who created the knowledge understand it far better than do most translators. They understand the nuances. They understand the caveats. The problem is that few academic scholars have much experience or training in public communication, and the academic culture has generally not supported academics being public. Fortunately, that is beginning to change, but oh so slowly.

I believe that academic scholars have a responsibility to be proactive in engaging directly with society. I believe that part of our obligation—our social contract, if you will—involves a two-way communication with society. Specifically, in exchange for public funding, our jobs are both to create new knowledge and to share it widely with transparency and humility. When I first proposed this idea of a social contract for science eighteen years ago in my presidential address, the academic culture was so chilling toward public engagement, I was pretty darn sure that I would have rotten tomatoes thrown at me when I gave my speech. However, much to my surprise and pleasure, I was given a standing ovation instead. I was told it was the first standing ovation that an American Association for the Advancement of Science (AAAS) presidential address had garnered. I took it as the beginning of a new awakening within the academic community. The culture was starting to shift, and people were more receptive than I thought they might be.

Since that time, I've seen the culture of academia continue to change—none too soon, in my view. Consider just the environment for a moment: the pace of change, the scale of change, and the kinds of environmental changes are unprecedented in human history. Those changes and the consequences that they have for human health, prosperity, equity, and well-being mean that we no longer have the luxury of waiting years to decades for new information to work its way into public understanding and political decision making. New knowledge and understanding are needed much sooner. Although there are indeed those who are resistant to hearing about certain topics, I have found great interest, curiosity, and receptivity among the public, business leaders, and many elected officials about scientific knowledge that's relevant to their interests and their problems. Many people want information, and in fact, they're often hungry for it, but they want something they can understand, they can trust, and they can use. In my experience, they put a lot of trust in academic scholars. However, in general, the academic community is not able to deliver those things that the public wants.

Here is our opportunity. Yes, it is fraught with danger, but that doesn't mean we should stick our heads in the sand. So let's consider why academics are so ambivalent about public engagement. I have compiled seven reasons, many of which were undoubtedly in your discussions earlier today:

1. We fear failure. We have witnessed colleagues who have not succeeded in sharing their knowledge accurately, and we don't want to be similarly misquoted, taken out of context, or made to look silly.
2. We lack the skills to translate complex information into simpler but still accurate information.
3. We're uncomfortable with modes of communication that are effective in public communication—storytelling, using analogies and metaphors, talking about ourselves.

4. We fear our colleagues will criticize us for seeking glory by having our names in the media or label us as the (dreaded) Advocate. (That's spelled with a scarlet letter *A*!)
5. We don't want to take time away from the things that count in the academic world—writing proposals, doing research, publishing results, or teaching.
6. We believe that public engagement will not be recognized as important in promotion and tenure decisions.
7. We fear criticism from activists who conduct aggressive campaigns against scholars with whom they disagree.

In my view, these are all valid concerns, but they stack up on the side of "why not" without equal consideration to "why yes" or, equally important, how some of the hurdles can be overcome.

Moreover, the urgency of many of the challenges facing society is driving more and more academics to feel an obligation to be more engaged—witness your conference. Even when those academics—and there are more and more of them—are successful at public engagement, they will often advise their own undergraduates and graduate students to focus first on their studies and their research and defer any public engagement until after tenure. Their advice goes, "Establish your credentials first. Solidify your academic position before doing things that are risky."

But by and large, the younger generation is not listening to that advice. They feel keenly invested in being part of the solution, not perpetuating the problem, and they want to use their knowledge, not just be hidden away in the ivory tower. Their values differ from those of many of their elders, and they are seeking ways to have meaningful careers that entail engagement.

Let me be very clear about one key issue here. I'm not suggesting that each and every academic scholar needs to be publicly engaged, only that more academics be engaged and that they be actively supported by all of us. Not every one of us is well suited to public communication, for example, but we should all support our colleagues who are, and—this is crucial—our institutions should support them as well.

One clear need is for more and better training programs to assist those interested in mastering bilingual and other engagement skills. Faculty and students alike are seeking such programs, but not enough good options exist. Many "media training" workshops (including those offered by universities) are typically conducted by communications experts, not by science communication experts. Those workshops can help scientists learn some of the requisite skills but are usually insensitive to scientists' values and culture and unable to help scientists figure out how to translate complex findings into something understandable or identify accurate metaphors or analogies. In my view, the whole package is needed.

My cofounders and I created the Leopold Leadership Program to provide training specifically for academic scientists. The COMPASS program, which I also cofounded, provided the all-important scientific communications training component. The Leopold Leadership Program also provides leadership and engagement training and was designed to grow a network of colleagues who could support one another and begin to change the academic culture; it targets midcareer academic environmental scientists.

Again, I was pleasantly surprised by the readiness of academic scientists for such a program. When we first created the program in the mid-1990s, we were not sure that anybody would even apply, simply because being public was not widely valued by university faculty. Much to our delight, the very first group of applicants was large and included superb scientists from top-notch institutions. They said they were motivated to be more engaged with society despite the culture in their universities. Since 1999, there have been ten cohorts of approximately twenty scientists trained in the Leopold Leadership Program for a total of around two hundred now adept academic scientist communicators and role models. Many have created courses at their institutions to replicate their training for their students. And because quite a few of those Leopold Leadership Fellows are now deans or directors or active leaders in their own institutions, they are actively working to change the culture.

COMPASS has honed its communication offerings and now offers a range of superb options for multiple academic stages, from graduate students through full professors, for both academic and conservation organizations. COMPASS helps scientists engage and engage effectively by training, coaching, and connecting them. Nancy Baron, the Director of Science Outreach at COMPASS, is with you and can provide more information about who COMPASS is, what they do, and why it has been so successful.

Both the Leopold and the COMPASS programs are in high demand as more and more academics seek to hone their skills. More and more university administrators appreciate the value of the training but struggle to find ways to fund these and other effective training programs.

Many of the elements of the COMPASS training parallel my own experiences about what makes for effective communication. Here are five tips:

1. Know your audience—who they are, what they care about, and what they know about your subject.
2. Answer the "so what?" question. Why should anyone care about what you're telling him or her? Why is it important? Whom does it affect?
3. Learn to translate complex scientific concepts and findings into plain language that is understandable but also accurate.
4. Use metaphors and analogies to help folks connect the dots from the known to the related unknown.
5. Tell stories. Social scientists tell us that stories are sticky. People remember them; hence they are very effective communication tools. Moreover, making it personal can help make you more accessible, less of a "nerdy" scientist, and even more credible.

With that in mind, let me tell you a couple of stories about communicating scientific information during my NOAA days.

My first story deals with the importance of knowing what your audience knows and starting from there. Here's the relevant background information you need for context: The National Weather Service, part of NOAA, relies on multiple sources of information to make weather forecasts, including weather balloons, ground radar stations, oceanic buoys, and satellites. Among these, satellites loom large: over 90 percent of the data that go into the numerical weather models come from weather satellites. When I arrived at NOAA, I learned the satellites we had in space were functioning well, but the program to build the next generation of weather satellites had been dysfunctional for some time. It was imperative we fix the program, so we did. The next step was to communicate to members of Congress how we fixed it and to urge that they provide funding now that things were in order. I vividly recall meeting with one member of Congress who was on a key committee, describing to him how important these weather satellites were and how important it was to fund them. He listened for a short time, then looked at me and said, "Doctor, I don't need your weather satellites. I've got the Weather Channel!" At that, I thought, "Oh, brother!" I obviously misjudged what he knew and had to take a few steps back and communicate to him that the Weather Channel, AccuWeather, and all the other private weather providers get their information from NOAA and that NOAA's weather satellites provide the bulk of the observations. Without NOAA's weather satellites, he wouldn't have the Weather Channel. Communication 101—know your audience. Know what they know about something, and then move from there, from the known to the related unknown.

My second story is about finding the right analogies in communicating science. Again, first some context. NOAA is one of the lead federal agencies producing, sharing, and assessing scientific information about climate change. NOAA keeps the climate records, leads the National Climate Assessment, hosts Climate.gov, produces new climate knowledge, and shares information about climate change and climate variability widely. As administrator, I received a lot of questions about climate change: some friendly, some seeking information, some antagonistic. I recall one congressional hearing where the topic du jour was the ten-year period of time called the "pause" or the "hiatus" in which we thought there had been no detectable change in the global average temperature. (New information has now shown the hiatus to be an artifact.) And at the hearing, a number of members of the committee asked, "Doctor, isn't it true that the global average temperature of the planet has not changed in the last ten years?" I replied, "Yes, Mr. Representative, that's what the data show." "Well, then, Doctor, isn't it true that climate change isn't happening?" And I replied something like, "Ten years is not a long enough period of time to detect a meaningful trend in a system that's very complex and very noisy." That answer was expected and didn't seem to make any difference to the questioners. Then I would have another individual ask me pretty much the same question. When a member who I knew was a surfer posed essentially the same question, I tried a different tack. I said to him, "Congressman, have you ever stood on a beach and watched ten waves coming ashore? Could you tell me, based on those ten waves, if the tide was going out or if it was coming in?" And he said, "No, of course not. Ten waves is not enough." Then he became silent, connecting the dots. He understood the analogy. His later public statements have suggested he has not changed his mind about climate change, most likely because for him it's not really a scientific or an evidence-based issue but rather a political one. But I think that analogy was useful to many people who were at the hearing because they could understand better why ten years is not long enough to detect a meaningful trend in the climate record. Finding a good analogy can be very, very helpful.

My third and final story also focuses on climate change and analogies. Context: Hurricane Sandy triggered a plethora of questions about the relationship between that superstorm and climate change: "Is this a harbinger of things to come? Was Sandy caused by climate change?" I was asked this over and over. Many scientists at the time were answering that question by talking about attribution and the challenges of attributing any single event to climate change. In my experience, when people hear a word like "attribution" that they don't understand, they tune out, distrust the information, or react negatively. So when I was asked that question, I responded with a baseball analogy. I would say, "When a baseball player starts taking steroids, the chances of his hitting home runs suddenly increase dramatically. Not only does he hit more homers, but more powerful ones. Everyone knows one cannot point to any particular home run and say, 'Aha, that home run is because he is taking steroids,' but the pattern that you're seeing of more and bigger homers is understood to be attributable to steroids. In similar fashion, what we are seeing on earth today is weather on steroids—weather on climate steroids. We are seeing more, longer-lasting heat waves, more intense storms, more droughts, and more floods. Those patterns are what we expect with climate change." For many people, that analogy is very helpful.

One of the most difficult aspects of this communication is figuring out how to translate very complicated scientific information into English without losing accuracy. No analogy, no metaphor, is perfect, but working to find the right ones is very worthwhile. Also, figuring out how to talk about something that's complicated in plain language is important. The COMPASS team is highly skilled at coaching scientists to do both.

Again, I would caution you that learning to become bilingual is much more than what is typically offered in "media training." It takes skilled trainers who understand the science to help scientists find accurate but understandable ways of talking about things in ways that audiences understand. And it's important that trainers understand the culture of science. Most media training offered by universities and by others doesn't meet either bar.

For anyone interested in science communications, I urge you to read Nancy Baron's book *Escape from the Ivory Tower*. She treats this issue in some depth and very eloquently.

I mentioned earlier that "engagement" to me means more than translation, more than sharing what you know with others. Engagement implies a two-way interaction. It means listening, not just talking. Moreover, there may well be benefit in both directions! I've witnessed some fascinating shifts in the problems that scholars are tackling because they are listening to the

concerns and questions of laypeople and have been motivated to seek answers that they were not previously researching.

For example, my colleagues and I had articulated in the mid- to late 1990s the need for more fully protected Marine Protected Areas (MPAs) to protect biodiversity and recover depleted fisheries. Marine resource managers and NGOs listened and said, "OK, we understand MPAs are important. How big do they need to be? How many do we need? How far apart should they be? Where should they be?" We scientists didn't have answers to those questions. A number of us realized that these were really important questions, and if we put our minds to it, we should be able to come up with good answers. So we put together a working group at the National Center for Ecological Analysis and Synthesis (NCEAS), a National Science Foundation–sponsored synthesis center affiliated with the University of California at Santa Barbara. We convened an interdisciplinary team of scientists and challenged ourselves to be more useful in providing answers to practical questions. Lo and behold, we came up with what has now become really useful guidance about "how many," "how big," and "how far apart" for creating fully protected marine reserves.

That guidance was inspired by societal needs, but it required fundamental advances in science. That type of science does not, therefore, fit cleanly into either the "applied science" or the "basic science" paradigm. It was not "applied science," which often means using existing knowledge and applying it in a new situation. Nor was it "basic science," which is curiosity driven. Donald Stokes would call what we did "use-inspired science." In his book *Pasteur's Quadrant,* he points out that the classic formulation of basic and applied science does not fully describe the spectrum of research. He proposes this third category of "use-inspired science" as fundamental, cutting-edge science that is responsive to society's needs. I think we're seeing an amazing proliferation of use-inspired science in almost all arenas of science, but especially around the topics of sustainability science, resource use, energy, health, and much more.

One very real reason to be more engaged with society, then, is also to be challenged by society—to be exposed to the kinds of questions whose answers might, in fact, be helpful to society.

Hence "engagement" is a rich endeavor for scientists. There really is a two-way exchange of information and perspectives. It's not just scientists communicating in one direction—that is, just sharing knowledge with laypeople. It's also scientists listening and being inspired to solve other problems that might not have been on their radar screen.

One of the toughest issues for many academic scholars who choose to engage with society is where they should engage along the spectrum of very low-risk to very high-risk activities. Becoming involved in K–12 education, citizen science, or public lectures is a lot less risky but still very useful. At the opposite end of the risky spectrum is outright advocacy for a particular solution. This is what I call the "scarlet letter of the scientific world": advocacy. Scientists are conflicted on the topic of advocacy. On the one hand, they feel a moral obligation to help society deal with important issues, but on the other, they are simultaneously cautioned that tainting science with bias will undermine the credibility of science.

I can tell you that many scientists feel that they are not only scientists but citizens and that they have a right as citizens to express their opinions about the solutions that they think are the right ones based on their information but also their values. They say that they can do so in a way that's not confusing, that they can say, "OK, I'm wearing my scientist hat, and this is what the science says, and now I'm going to wear my citizen's hat, and this is my recommendation." The ability to distinguish which hat one is wearing makes scientists more comfortable about engaging in advocacy. However, in my experience, most laypeople and policy makers don't even hear the distinction between "this hat" and "that hat." They hear everything a scientist says and interpret it as scientific guidance (which of course contributes to confusion when scientists disagree with one another).

Other scientists say that any scientists who voice their own opinions undermine the credibility of all scientists. They believe that any advocacy will compromise all science. I would note that physicians are routinely advocates, and are expected to be, but do not lose their credibility in the process. Recommending that people not smoke or that they exercise does not seem to make physicians less credible. But the dialogue in the environmental science arena seems to have different rules.

This is a very rich dialog for which there is no single answer for all scientists or all academics. Many scientists choose a middle ground in which scientists offer useful, actionable input to policy makers without making overt recommendations. For example, one can say about climate change, "This is what we know, and based on our understanding of what we know, if we choose this path, this is the likely outcome. If we choose a different path, this is the likely outcome." So you can frame answers in the fashion of choices with consequences, in which you are not making overt recommendations but are focusing mostly on the scientific understanding. This, of course, is the "policy-relevant but not policy-proscriptive" approach taken by the Intergovernmental Panel on Climate Change (IPCC). But I would emphasize that which level of engagement you choose is a personal choice and that you need to think deeply about the issues and make a conscious decision.

It may be useful to consider history here. In past decades, the bulk of academic scientists have erred on the side of isolation to protect the objectivity of the ivory tower. Engagement was perceived as tarnishing the reputation of science. The reputation of science may well still be an issue, but the consequences of not engaging are far different today than in earlier times. The balance is shifting, with society more at risk and more in need of scientific knowledge, which is why you are having this discussion. Science has a meaningful role to play in charting the future of all people. Do we sit idly by and protect the integrity of science, or do we figure out how to minimize the negative consequences and engage wholeheartedly because it's our obligation to be helpful? Today, more and more scientists believe that the consequences of not engaging outweigh the consequences of engaging. If scientists don't engage, society does not have the benefit of the information scientists have that may be useful in addressing many of the most challenging issues of our time. I firmly believe that we need more scientifically informed citizens and policy makers and that science should be at the table informing the decisions they make. I believe that scientists should engage both in the public discourse and in the policy arena. I believe that scientists have an obligation to be helpful to society.

Thus far, we've explored a little bit about the "why," the "who," the "when," and the "how" to engage. I'm sure that you will pursue many of these topics, either in our Q&A or in your deliberations tomorrow. Engagement presents significant challenges and opportunities to academia; we've talked about some of the tradeoffs.

For many academics, engagement is a defining issue of our time. Bob Dylan's words are appropriate: "The times, they are a-changin'." I've personally witnessed a seismic shift in academics' attitudes toward public and political discourse, and importantly, I've seen a generational divide emerge as younger scientists find their voices and as their values differ from those of their elders. This is a critically important issue for the academic community to grapple with. The topic goes to the heart of the responsibilities of individuals and the academic community to society and how we can best be of service to society.

As a senior scientist, I don't believe that my students should follow the path that I took: establish your scientific credentials first and then begin to be more public. Those choices were informed and framed by different times. Engaging with society was not even on the radar screen of most academics when I began my career. Only as the environment began to change radically and neither the public nor policy makers were paying much attention did I begin to engage. When I did so, I felt I had to break away from academic conventions. Doing so was difficult, but it was the right thing to do. The world continues to change and to need scientists and scholars to help chart the future. I continue to feel compelled to both engage actively with society—on the public and policy fronts—and create pathways for others to do so. I feel strongly about the need for my generation to also champion the right of younger academics to chart their own paths along the continuum of engagement and to do so with their seniors' full support. I hope these thoughts have been useful to your deliberations. I would be delighted to engage in exchanges with you on these very important topics and wish you well in your deliberations over the next day and beyond. Thank you all very much. [Applause]

ANDREW MAYNARD: Before we take questions from the audience, I'm going to take my prerogative as moderator here to ask the first question. So you talked a lot about the personal responsibility and personal opportunities of individuals to engage. In your sense, how does that apply to institutions? Where do you feel the responsibility is for academic institutions like Michigan, for instance, to either support, or create infrastructure that supports, or encourage academics to be part of that public dialog?

JANE LUBCHENCO: Well, it won't surprise you, Andrew, to hear that I think institutions have an obligation to create the reward structures, platforms, and training opportunities for their students and faculty to engage in the world. In my experience, universities have been much more willing to do that than have the faculty, who have been more resistant. Universities like to see their faculty and their students profiled and quoted in newspapers. They like to see them engage. They like to be able to tell the citizens of the state and their funders that their faculty and students are being useful and relevant. Universities per se are not the stumbling block; the faculty is. Faculty are much more risk averse and are not, as a body, as willing to be engaged as maybe the institution would like them to be. This is what needs to change. I would like to see faculty empower themselves and their students to be active on both public and policy fronts but find ways to do so that minimize (not eliminate) problems.

QUESTION 1, ANDREW HOFFMAN (UNIVERSITY OF MICHIGAN): Jane, I found your comments extremely valuable. But your career brings something different to this conversation. You actually stepped out of academia into politics and then from politics back into academia. Can you talk about the challenges? And there must have been costs in doing that. It must have been hard to reengage the research agenda after being in the political arena for however many years you were there. Can you talk about those transitions and the challenges of doing that?

JANE LUBCHENCO: Let's see; where to begin? Let me first say that early in my career I was just doing my research, publishing, teaching—doing the typical things that academics do. I became

involved in the Ecological Society of America—in an activity designed to help articulate to funders, Congress, and funding agencies the importance of ecological research with the idea of attracting more funding for that, because it was pretty much abysmal at the time. The result was the Sustainable Biosphere Initiative, which really charted a new direction for the field of ecology. It said that there should be two criteria for determining research priorities: areas on the cutting edge of science and areas that were relevant to societal needs. And we identified climate change, ecological causes and consequences of biodiversity, and ecological causes and consequences of sustainability as priority topics for funding for ecological research and then connected the dots for people between what some would think of as very basic esoteric science and how making progress in those areas was actually relevant to societal interests. So the message was that relevance was not a four-letter word. After we did that, there was intense interest on the part of members of Congress, various committees, Congressional Budget Office, Office of Management and Budget, and the funding agencies in learning more about the benefits of funding more ecological research. And it quickly became obvious that there were very few scientists on the committee and very few academic ecologists who were able to talk about the science and its relevance in ways that people understood. And that partly led to creation of the Leopold Leadership Program and COMPASS. But it also led to my being more public and engaged more in Washington, DC. So by the time President Obama asked me to go lead NOAA in 2008, I had actually spent a fair amount of time in Washington testifying before congressional committees on a range of topics (science funding, biodiversity, climate change, and other things). I had been president of AAAS and the Ecological Society of America and served on the National Science Foundation's board of directors, the National Science Board, and multiple National Academy of Sciences committees. So when I went to NOAA in 2009, it wasn't quite the same as many academics just being plunked from the academic world into the political world. I actually had a lot of experience in that world and could draw on that. I knew, probably, thirty members of Congress personally; we had done a lot of things together on a range of topics. I knew a lot of people in agencies, and so even though I had never been in government, I was not completely naïve. I joked that being a marine biologist was really good training for the rough-and-tumble world of politics because I already knew how to swim with sharks. But there is actually an element of truth to that, because a lot of what you learn as a scientist is actually more applicable than you might think to the world of politics. But you do have to figure out the culture. So my transition to the world of government was not as abrupt or jarring as might have been the case otherwise.

I found it very rewarding to be a public servant. I think that it is important for academics to take their turn and work for the government. Many of you serve on various advisory committees and in other advisory roles; that's really important. But to be a government official is a different kind of public service that I think is also incredibly important, incredibly valuable. I never thought of becoming a permanent government employee. A lot of people go to Washington, get seduced by it, and want to stay. Not me. My reasons were in part personal. During the four years I was there, my husband, Bruce, was back in Oregon. He had agreed to take over the research we had been doing together and advise the students we had coadvised so that I could go to DC without giving up thirty years' worth of long-term data that we have for our studies' sites or leaving my students in the lurch. But I never had any intention of staying there, and coming back after four years seemed like a very reasonable thing to do. It wasn't soon enough in Bruce's view. You know, he was wishing I had come back after two years. It really is a sacrifice, but I think it's an important one.

I don't think there were insurmountable costs to my career. I continued to publish, to find active ways to connect the science that we were doing at NOAA, and to highlight insights from that by way of publications. And so I didn't have a four-year gap in my publication record, for example. One downside: I did have to give up all my grants. I'm starting from scratch now and reacquiring funding to support activities and research. So that is a cost, but it was one I was willing to bear. Coming back to academia, I think I've actually benefited hugely from the experiences that I've had in government. I teach classes now about the Science Policy Interface to help students understand better how their science actually is used, perceived, or portrayed in the policy world. I think that's really useful to scientists who are really interested in having their science be relevant. So I think it has added significant value.

I would strongly urge any of you who have an opportunity to serve in a similar capacity to say yes! But do it with your eyes open. Don't go there to be a caretaker. Too many folks do, and it's a waste. I went to DC with a very ambitious agenda, and despite the very challenging circumstances, we accomplished an impressive amount. We had the oil spill, a dysfunctional weather satellite program, the most extreme weather of any four years in US history, "Climategate" and the intense politicization of climate science, and a dysfunctional Congress that was policy light and partisan heavy. So we had many, many challenges, but we were able to accomplish a huge amount, among them NOAA's new Scientific Integrity Policy—a landmark policy that will serve it well. It says it is not permissible to distort, suppress, manipulate, or cherry-pick the science. And it allows scientists at NOAA to speak freely to the media without going through a gatekeeper, which is highly unusual for a federal agency. We also turned the corner in ending overfishing in the United States and are on a path to rebuilding fisheries in a way that a lot of people said would not be possible, and we've demonstrated that it is. We fixed the problematic weather satellite program. We helped create the first National Ocean Policy and much more. I feel really proud that we were able to do so much. It was a great experience to work alongside the very talented civil servants at NOAA who are really dedicated to their jobs. So overall, it was very rewarding, though from day to day I certainly cycled through a full spectrum of emotions. I was in turns frustrated, ecstatic, depressed, and euphoric. But in the end, I'm really glad I did it.

QUESTION 2, JENNIFER CHERRIER (FLORIDA A&M UNIVERSITY): Thank you very much for a very inspirational and elegant presentation, and I also thank you for your service. My question to you is, I'm curious about your perspective about scientists engaging with the private sector. What do you think about that?

JANE LUBCHENCO: I tend to think of different communities that scientists might engage with. The private sector is definitely one of them. NGOs, civil society, government, and media are other communities. And I think it's important for scientists to engage with all of them, but doing so means investing some time and energy to understand the culture and the values of that community and figuring out how to engage in a way that is helpful but does not compromise you. And that's true regardless of which of those communities you're working with. There are some NGOs, for example, that I would engage with quite readily and others that I wouldn't touch with a ten-foot pole. And the criterion, the first criterion for me, is whether they respect science and scientists and whether they are going to be open and listen to information or whether they're going to abuse the information or you. And that concern is equally valid whether it's an NGO, or a journalist, or somebody in the private sector. So I think the same applies to all those communities.

It's more difficult for most scientists to engage with the private sector because there are fewer points of intersection, but not all businesses, not all industries, are the same. I have seen some interactions with the private sector that are actually very productive and very useful. I have seen some that just are a disaster. So I think the rules of engagement are important. I think that you need to have a clear understanding of what each party is bringing to the table, what each wants, what the timetable is, who owns the information, what the expectations are, for example, around data ownership and publishing. You know, there is a whole range of questions.

One example I've seen of successful engagement with the private sector is what the Natural Capital Project is doing. This is a group of scientists and experts that are based at Stanford, University of Minnesota, the World Wildlife Fund, and The Nature Conservancy. They are focused on understanding better and quantifying the benefits that ecosystems provide the people, figuring out how to understand the trade-offs and different uses of ecosystems, and then plugging that into policy or management decisions. So they have teamed up with some in the private sector who own land to think about managing that land for particular ecosystem services—water purification, for example, or water delivery. So there can be very productive interactions. It's perfectly appropriate for scientists to engage with any one of those communities, but it takes time and energy to really figure out how to do it in a way that works for everybody. And so I would say, go into it with your eyes open, do some pilots first, talk to other people, figure out what their experiences have been, and figure out not just whether to do it but how to do it in a way that would be successful.

QUESTION 3, HON. BRIAN BAIRD (4PIR2 COMMUNICATIONS): I have a two-part question, mostly so you can pick one or the other. One is the general concern we've heard today about the general public skepticism about science in general. We see it about climate but also vaccines and so on, and I'd appreciate your insights into how to address that. A second, maybe more difficult, question is, what are your thoughts about when scientists are faced with very controversial and politically sensitive decisions where there are no right or wrong answers, such as the president's decision to allow drilling in the Arctic, which may contradict a lot of marine scientists' perspectives? Clearly this is something where there's going to be a lot of passion, a lot of uncertainty. What is the role of academics there? I'd welcome your thoughts on one or either of those.

JANE LUBCHENCO: Brian, it's great to hear your voice. Thank you for all your public service over the years, and it was a real pleasure to work with you when you were in Congress. So great to see you.

I think one of the biggest issues with the skepticism about science is that it all boils down to trust. And in arenas like climate science, where there has been so much hype, so much poisoning of the waters by climate deniers, it is very difficult for most people to sort out what's happening and what they should believe. Most people tend to go to someone that they know, someone who

shares their values. And they're more likely to trust someone who shares their values than someone who is just some scientist someplace. So this really points to the importance of having and tapping into relationships and the importance of scientists connecting with natural communities of people who share their values. I would highlight Katharine Hayhoe, who is a climate scientist and a deeply religious person who has been able to make very significant inroads with the fundamentalist Christian community who shares her values because she talks to them in a language that acknowledges their values and also is able to share scientific information. One of the challenges of global communication about issues like climate is that it really gets devoid of, or divorced from, individual communicators. And that's a challenge.

In my experience, most people are hungry for information. To be sure, there is a subset of people that see climate change just as a knee-jerk political issue, but in my experience, a lot of the public is actually just confused about whom to believe. Many of them are now changing their minds about it because they've seen all this weird weather and, rightly or wrongly, they think that's because of climate change. And so it's gone out of the realm of science and into the realm of their own personal experience, and that is changing things. But I think it really underscores the importance of trust and people communicating with others that they can trust. And I see Skip [Arthur] Lupia is there. The social scientists have taught us a huge amount about communication of scientific information. And we need to listen to them a lot more than was the case early on.

The second issue that you raised, Brian, has to do with political choices that are not really about the science. Those choices can be informed by the science, but they involve a whole range of other issues—in this case, politics or economics and who knows what else. To drill in the Arctic or not is not really a scientific decision, and a lot of political decisions are not scientific decisions. Science can inform them, but as I mentioned earlier, those decisions are going to be based on other factors. And I think scientists need to really understand that these are choices that society, a president, or a member of Congress is making. My hope is that those choices will be appropriately informed by the science. But I don't think we should fool ourselves that someone who is listening to the science is automatically going to choose what you would choose. That underscores the importance of people weighing in and what they believe. But they shouldn't frame it just around science; they should also frame it around their own values if they are weighing in as citizens.

ANDREW MAYNARD: Jane, just to follow up on that, because I think it ties in very neatly—I have a question on a card that says, "It appears we're talking about two different kinds of discourse: public engagement and political engagement. The first is really looking at sort of academic expertise and scientific expertise and the second one is possibly looking more at personal values." I actually think from what you're saying that if you look at political engagement, there are two sides to that. The first side is informing political dialogue and the second one is actually taking a stance in a political debate. And I didn't know whether you wanted to talk a little bit more about where you see that line between what is acceptable as an academic or part of the academy as opposed to where you cross a line into personal advocacy.

JANE LUBCHENCO: I agree completely with what you said, Andrew, that in the political discourse there are two elements. One is providing scientific information to inform the dialogue. And the second is taking a stance, taking a position, making a specific recommendation based on both science and personal values. I believe that we should absolutely be providing that information and doing it in a way that understands how the political discourse happens, what the rules of engagement are, how it works, and the timeliness element. I believe that it is perfectly appropriate for scientists as individual citizens to also be acting on their values and urging particular actions. Just because they are scientists doesn't mean they relinquish their rights as citizens. But I think that they need to make it clear that they are acting on their values—informed by science but acting on their values. And I think that we need to be tolerant of that range of choices that individuals, individual academic scientists, can make within this political discourse realm: to choose either to just provide information or to provide information and take a stance.

QUESTION 4, AMY SCHALET (UNIVERSITY OF MASSACHUSETTS, AMHERST): I'm probably revealing my discipline as a sociologist or my upbringing in northern Europe, but when I was listening to your five values and the two additional ones that came after, I was waiting for something that would say something like that "science can help us promote equity," or social inclusion, or something along those lines. And I was curious to hear your reflections on a potential way of defending science or invoking its need, especially in light of the fact that some of the most pressing issues in American society today involve inequality, inequity, and so forth and that the discourse politically may actually be changing in favor of those issues and the issue of equality and inequality in America.

JANE LUBCHENCO: That's a great question. One of my "roles of science" was to improve our lives. And one could argue that equity is essential to improving lives—all of our lives. But I think a better answer is that what you're really focusing on is about values—about values of society,

about values of individuals—and that science, both natural and social science, can help us understand what equity means, how to achieve equity, what the tradeoffs are. But in the end, the choices about what to do to have a more equitable society are really about values. And it's not simply a matter for science or for scholarship. Scholarship and science can inform it, but in the end, it's really about values. And what Pope Francis, for example, is bringing to the table is a strong passion about the value of addressing these issues. Same with Senator Elizabeth Warren. Same with other champions who are focusing on equity. I would cite Thomas Piketty as a scholar who has helped us understand what the patterns of inequity have been within and across countries as a way that academic scholarship can help us understand the issues and show patterns. But in the end, it's going to be the choices of society, individuals, and institutions about this very important issue.

ANDREW MAYNARD: Well, Jane, thank you so much. That was enlightening, thought provoking, and thoroughly excellent. I'm not even going to apologize for the technology, because I think this actually worked exceptionally well. So thank you very much for your time. That's given us a lot to work on for the next few days.

JANE LUBCHENCO: Thank you. Good night. [Applause]

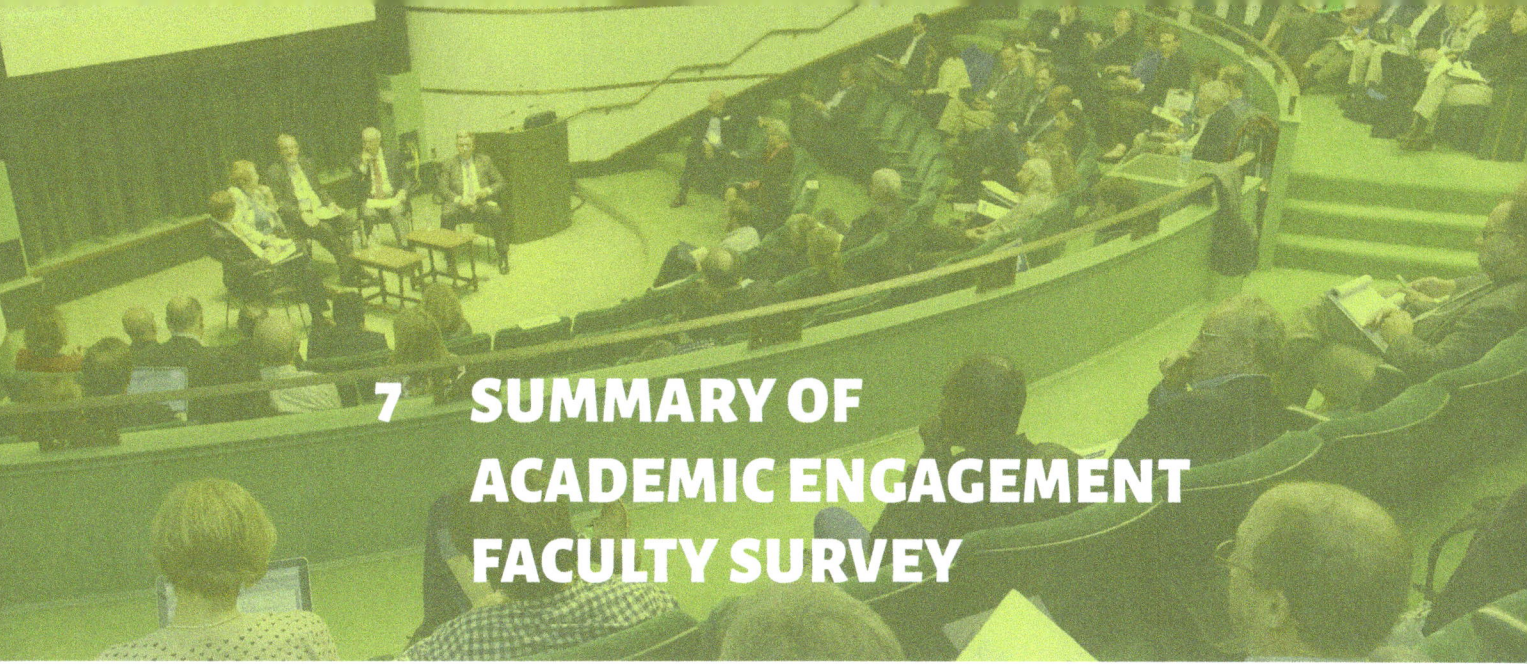

7 SUMMARY OF ACADEMIC ENGAGEMENT FACULTY SURVEY

Introduction

Should academics engage in public and political debates? To begin a discussion of this and the associated issues, we surveyed the actions and attitudes among University of Michigan (U-M) faculty between November 15 and 28, 2013. Results from this survey will inform a series of brownbag lunches where faculty can meet to discuss their experiences in engaging in public and political debates. With data collected from the survey and the brownbag lunches, we propose to organize a national conference at the University of Michigan that seeks to analyze the role that academics can and should play within public and political debates and, importantly, the opportunities, hazards, and best practices for doing so.

Respondents were recruited via e-mail, using the network of affiliates of the Erb Institute for Global Sustainable Enterprise; the Ross School of Business; the School of Natural Resources and Environment; the Energy Institute, Engineering; the Department of English; the School of Information; the Risk Science Center, School of Public Health; and the Graham Environmental Sustainability Institute. We administered the survey online using Qualtrics and analyzed the data with SPSS 22. There were 368 respondents in total, with roughly 330 usable responses.

This is a summary of our preliminary analysis, in which we answer each of our research questions: What types of public and political activities do faculty members undertake? What do they consider as being the opportunities and barriers in such activities? What do they consider as the role of the university in facilitating such activities? How do their beliefs, attitudes, and actions vary as a function of their sociodemographics?

As the aim of our research is the relative groupings of respondents' beliefs, attitudes, and actions and not the testing of hypotheses per se, we restrict the quantitative analyses to measuring simple frequencies and the strength of the association between variables.

Although these are self-selected respondents (i.e., a nonprobability sample), we attempt to determine if they appear representative of U-M faculty. While it is not our intent to generalize to larger populations, response bias is still a possible concern.[18] Thus we compare the sociodemographics of respondents with their departments to determine if there are broad trends in response and nonresponse. Of the respondents, 41 percent would be interested in participating in a series of brownbag lunches where scholars share their experiences in public and political engagement (35 percent maybe, 24 percent no).

1. Have you done or do you intend to do any of the following public and/or political engagement activities?

Over 62 percent of respondents give media interviews, 59 percent provide assistance to government agencies, and 59 percent give talks or presentations to the general public. Of the respondents, 39 percent do not, and never will, use Twitter for academic/professional work; 35 percent say the same for Facebook (though 58 percent use Twitter and Facebook for personal communication).

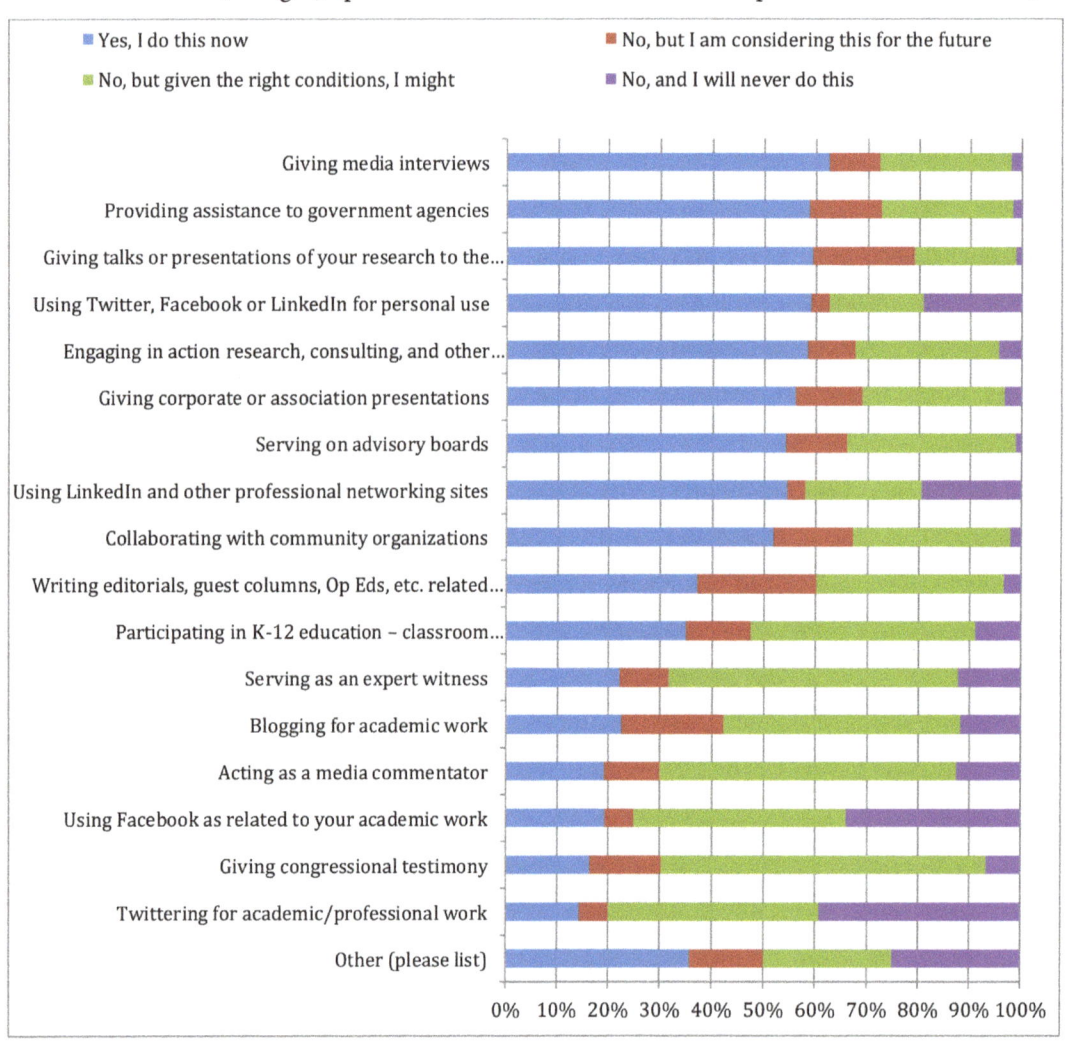

18. Though we lack overall faculty demographic data, our respondents appear to be more male (66 percent), older (31 percent are thirty years or more since their PhD; 49 percent are between fifty and seventy years old), and more senior than what might be expected in the general faculty population (72 percent are tenure-track; 30 percent are full professor). Also, we have high representation from certain schools/faculties (23 percent engineering, 18 percent law, 15 percent business, and 11 percent public health) and low representation in others (no representation from art and design, education, kinesiology, nursing, and pharmacy).

Other activities include the following:

- *Consulting:* For government and for nonprofit organizations
- *Creating online content:* A website to teach mathematics; online community events
- *Writing policy and standards:* NAS studies, SAE and ISO standards, white papers
- *Working with NGOs:* Volunteering, teaching, providing pro bono technical assistance, assisting with advocacy strategy, participating in various local community activities, working with international NGOs on reforms in developing countries, conducting collaborative research with community-based organization leaders (who in turn share research findings, for example, as expert witnesses and in congressional testimony)

2. To better understand why, please indicate how much you agree or disagree with the following statements.

Public/political engagement...

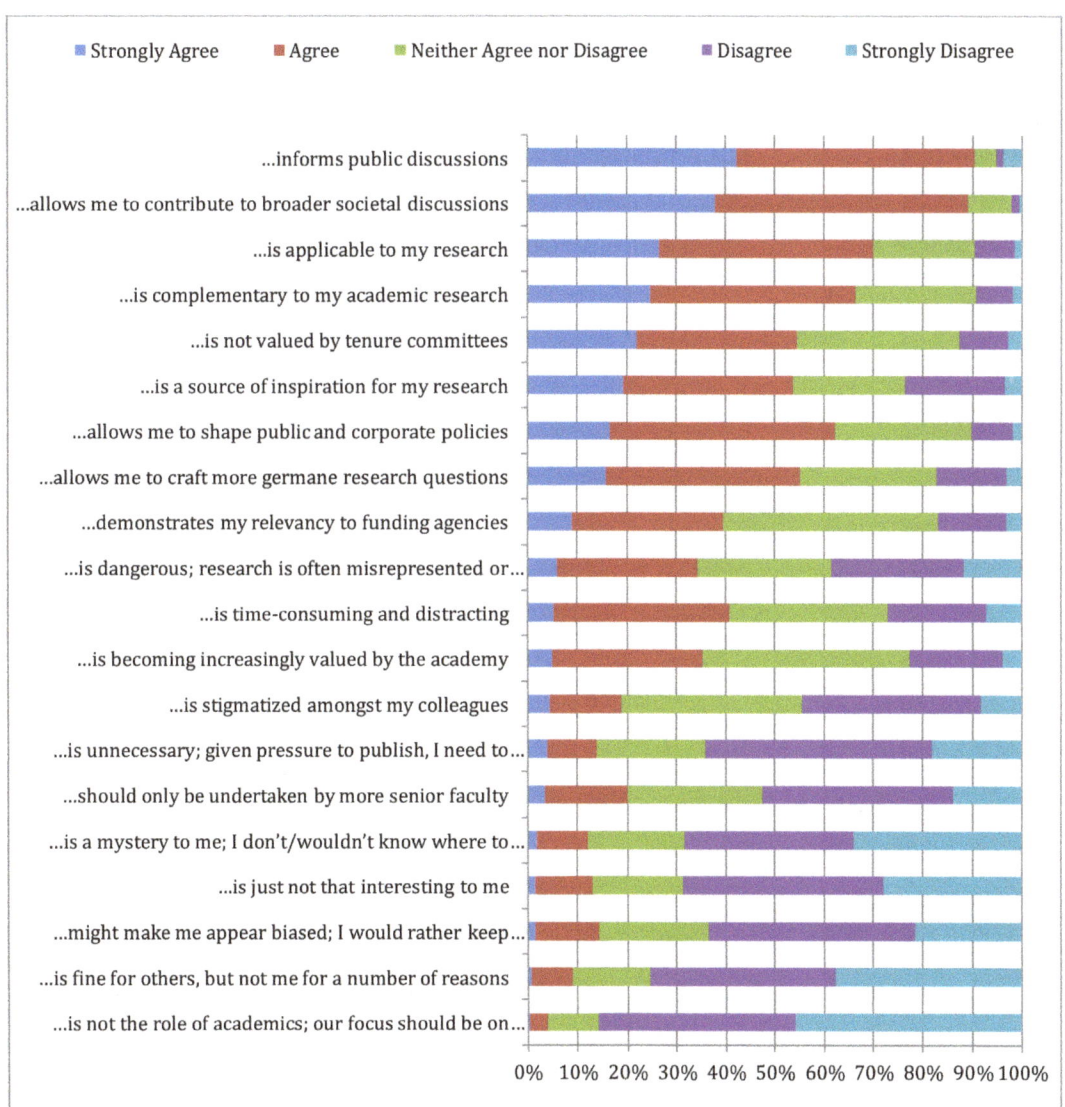

Of the respondents, 90 percent agree or strongly agree that public engagement informs public discussions, and 86 percent disagree or strongly disagree that this is not the role of academics. Sixty-six percent believe that external engagement is complementary to their academic research, though 56 percent believe this activity is not valued by tenure committees and 35 percent believe it is becoming increasingly valued by the academy. Thirty-four percent believe this activity is dangerous, as it is often misquoted, and 41 percent believe it is time consuming and distracting.

3. Any additional comments on the obstacles or incentives, hazards or opportunities to engaging in public and political discussion not listed above?

The respondents provided the following comments:

- It is surprisingly difficult to navigate this arena to find outlets that are an effective use of one's time. The *New York Times* is the gold standard, but even insiders have little idea how to get onto the op-ed page. Other newspapers (possibly excepting the *Wall Street Journal* and *Washington Post*) are of little value in reaching the public; beyond that, blogs and other platforms are likely to play mostly to the vanities of authors (which is also fine).
- There are twenty-four hours in a day.
- I worry that public engagement could make political enemies who could potentially interfere with my career for nonacademic reasons.
- Obstacles: Many faculty are not prepared to work with the media, for example (e.g., translating their research and its significance into sound bites). Some faculty still believe that faculty should not be involved in political engagement, and some faculty fear that doing so will diminish them in the eyes of important colleagues. I also think there's a jealousy component here: Those who don't do so may say they don't want to while not doing so because they fear their inadequacy.
- It is sometimes difficult for university people to achieve credibility with the public. There is often an assumption that they have narrow knowledge and do not understand "real-world" problems.
- Senior officials threaten when one speaks out about a concern that he or she sees, a concern that the person may have reported to the SEC, the IRS, and others.
- Could writing one's congressman (who is against increased funding for scientific research) be misinterpreted and bring more scrutiny to the university?
- The "hazards" vary widely depending on the channel of communications. Blogs, testimony, presentations, and so on permit one to get a complete message out there. One has much less control in dealing with the press, whose objective is often a sound bite that may be out of context, misquoted, or misconstrued.
- Most faculty live in a bubble and appear naïve and out of touch when discussing something not directly related to their research. Because I view political activities as being outside of a faculty member's job description, I believe faculty should engage in political discussions to the same extent that other citizens do (no more, no less) and not in the context of their jobs.
- Not all who received this survey are evaluated according to the same metrics. Distinguishing respondents by type of professorial appointment (e.g., tenure-track, clinical, lecturer,

research) might give a more accurate picture. I am clinical faculty, so much of my public engagement directly supports how my work is perceived by my leadership.

- This survey is poorly designed. You are conflating two different things. The "communication of that research" is fine and indeed the responsibility of every academic. On the other hand, advocating public policies is the very opposite of science and objective research. For example, if one studies climate, describing the research is great, but advocating for carbon taxes is anti-scientific and will undermine the academy over the long run. When one begins advocating a specific public policy, one can no longer claim to have no stake in the outcome of objective research and thus no claim to objective science.
- I think the wording of these questions is terrible! You have set up the questions as if there is a dichotomy between outreach versus research, and many of your questions incorrectly equate measurable consequences of outreach (e.g., it is "time-consuming") with value judgments (e.g., it is "distracting"). I think your survey is foul and misleading. Many of the pros and cons are simultaneously true.
- My school places reasonable value on this activity, so I don't feel particularly conflicted between what I know I should do and what I do to make a committee happy.
- There is pressure from corporate partners and donors to the university not to engage in advocacy.
- There is a danger of being misrepresented and then subject to harassment, particularly online.
- I'm not eligible for tenure, so it could result in the loss of my job.
- It's important not to be a hack, and that risk is a real one.
- Science is often miscommunicated by laymen and incorrectly presented as fact to the public (of course, oftentimes also out of a political bias—so on purpose). Certainly, scientists would principally be really qualified to communicate science to the public. *But* this is a very dangerous business, as the media often times take quotes out of context, so one has to be very careful not to do more harm than good. Also, as faculty, we are not really trained to do this.
- Government agencies, courts, and the media are more interested in partisan positions than in balanced analysis. They seem to feel that the best way to get a balanced analysis is to present and compare two unbalanced views.
- All of my responses above need to be taken in the context that I am emeritus, eighty-six years old, and still active (and will be as long as health permits).
- The emotional impact of negative comments and personal attacks received after publishing/posting in public can be severe and hard to cope with. In public engagement related to climate change, the large majority of responses from anonymous members of the public are denialist, often personal, bitter, and angry. It's hard not to get caught up in responding, but that usually starts an endless cycle that's hard to get out of.
- The "I do it now" category I took to mean "I do it now or have done it in the recent past."
- Public engagement is important but needs to done carefully for the reasons stated above (being misquoted, unfairly criticized, etc.).
- It's strongly discouraged in engineering and exact sciences, particularly in young faculty.
- If you want faculty to engage with the public, it must be structurally rewarded in hiring and promotion, just like research.

- Often the people who are engaging with the public seem to be precisely the ones who ought least to be doing so, at least in my opinion. I think more engagement would lead to better than average engagement, but then I wonder, who am I to say that my views are the right ones?
- It's easy for the commentators to make a newbie academic look like a fool. This makes it difficult to get started. Once you are seen as a fool, it's difficult to get anyone to take you seriously.
- Those who generated this survey seem completely paranoid to me. Either that or they are just afraid of or do not understand technology. As an engineer, I see my role in society as becoming increasingly important. The politicians are not going to solve the world's problems. Engineers need to be much more strongly engaged.
- While funding agencies (specifically federal) often have members of the public engaged in part of the process, the actual merit scoring of most grants in my field pays essentially no attention to public engagement or opinion. I have seen this as both an applicant and a reviewer.
- Time is limited.
- Writing design standards and policies need to be considered in tenure decisions just as journal articles are considered.
- I think the real danger here is the underlying assumption that already pervades this questionnaire—that is, that academics as a group should do more public engagement. I think that is wrongheaded. Academia always had various functions and roles. Some academics served a public role; some did basic research. This is true even today. We have Richard Dawkins, Neil deGrasse Tyson, Paul Krugman, Melissa Harris-Perry, and Chomsky, to name but a few. Substitute those names with perhaps Sagan, Dewey, or Thomas Huxley and one gets examples of public academics of the past. This is a very good separation of labor. It is not actually true that we need more professors to spend less time doing research and more time being public figures. In fact, time to do actual research is already limited for professors due to the level of demands for teaching, grant writing, and service. We need those who do public outreach to be excellent at what they do. And we need those who actually do serious research to have the time to do it! However, there are very real negative consequences already because this narrative of public discourse is being propagated. The quality of job talks is more frequently close to public relations TED talks rather than serious discussions of deep, intellectual work. Being in the media often is seen as a pathway to tenure, and it is not at all a pathway that is problematic. Flashy, widely visible results trump hard work in the lab that does not have the same PR. All these are very troubling developments and should not be encouraged but countered. Aspects of this are not new either, as sociologist Pierre Bourdieu has already investigated in the 1980s. Public visibility has long been a mechanism to accrue academic status. If we require this of everybody, however, we lose out on the potential to nurture great minds who do not have the talent for public discourse.
- Untenured faculty whom I have spoken with sometimes have a great fear of saying anything that might be controversial or not "politically correct."
- I coauthored a report you might like to look at: *Scholarship in Public: Knowledge Creation and Tenure Policy in the Engaged University* (Ellison and Eatman, 2008). I would be delighted

to participate in work addressing this issue (http://imaginingamerica.org/fg-item/scholarship-in-public-knowledge-creation-and-tenure-policy-in-the-engaged-university/).
- The polarization of public discourse creates the hazard that the scholar may be identified as a politically partisan.
- I find society in general lacks open-minded discourse, and legal ramifications dissuade me from being actively engaged. The university's institutionalized bias of nonmainstream thoughts and values further discourages open discussion. It is not obvious to me that the university community even recognizes the narrow spectrum of its institutionalized culture.
- Many use the perception that this work is risky to avoid making public contributions. However, I don't think this kind of work is for everyone. There are many in academia who don't have the kind of interests or personality to work well with the lay public. Good public work requires the ability to listen, learn, and collaborate.
- I have always taken the policy advocacy approach rather than the neutral expert approach and have been involved in national and international policy debates and political decisions through congressional testimony and white papers. This action-oriented research is not as highly valued by the academy as some other types, but it is profoundly more interesting.
- Major concerns involve trying to communicate with people who have such different world views and educational levels that it is difficult to argue effectively.
- Tenure and academic incentives do not encourage public engagement.
- I'm not sure how necessary this is, but lest there be any perceived conflict of interest or partisan interests, I take a lot of care to ensure that my public engagement is done on my own time and with my own resources. I do spend substantial time in public engagement, and it helps that I have a 50 percent appointment.
- A tremendous amount of energy is required to make sure that my words are not misinterpreted. I have also had major media outlets plagiarize my own words without attributing them to me. For example, Nancy Schneiderman of NBC plagiarized my own term "misguided benevolence" without attribution.
- This is something that as academics we can and should do. Many of us have. But we should also resist being co-opted by for-profit entities. This is a big danger, and I think the university should really think twice about the ways that its faculty might end up getting used in unsavory ways.
- There are many roles for academics in public/political engagement. Such engagement does not have to mean advocacy, and I work hard to maintain discernable objectivity. As a result of this, I am regularly asked to, say, write a blog prior to governmental meetings, because blogs are entered into public testimony, and mine are viewed as more objective than most. What I write does not help me with funding agencies; in fact, I could probably argue that it hurts me, because program managers are concerned with what I might say. I often say I could not have the level of engagement that I have if I did not have tenure.
- It takes time and energy, which may detract from work toward tenure.
- More talk . . . The whole higher education system is an anachronism. The best research and teaching content is almost never in academic journals any longer, and for various reasons. The biggest reason is that there is a veritable tsunami of content being published in myriad different media. In both scale and scope, peer-reviewed research is a single, tiny piece of mist

- coming off of that tidal wave. Universities fret that massive open online courses threaten their franchise, and indeed they do. But this is only one franchise that is in peril. And the fundamentals driving the tsunami are incontrovertible and unstoppable. The die is cast.
- Our research needs to relate to the world; this is so basic. In medicine, we do research to solve problems (e.g., disease) and promote health. Likewise, in social sciences (including topics like economics), we need to relate to the world and help improve it (fix problems and promote well-being). In both, there is basic research that might be more esoteric and ivory tower *and* work that is more closely related to phenomena. In either case, there needs to be dialogue and interactions beyond the academy to inform research questions and share research processes and findings. The only hazard I see is being isolated and removed from society.
- Not all interactions are the same—in terms of skills required, potential benefits to the community/discourse, and potential for negative consequences (time consumption, potential for public, legal, or academic attack). There is not much training in this or guidance on how to choose the best forums.
- I am currently pretenure and am not doing a lot of public or political engagement. After tenure, I'd be more open to pursuing opportunities of this kind.
- Lecturers should be a part of this discussion, but they face a different set of pressures regarding time, emphasis on teaching and teaching evaluations for continued contracts, and a set of time constraints in which research and communication may not be factored into job descriptions or performance reviews.
- The push for an increase in this aspect of our work must come from "the top" and then be backed up all the way down the leadership chain into the schools, the departments, and advice regarding tenure preparations. Also, it would be good to have better tools and training on how to approach these discussions. The University of Michigan does not do this very well as compared to some top professional schools.
- On one hand, being too focused on influencing the public discourse will derail an academic scholar from the important research work he or she needs to do. On the other hand, the more our public policy gets out of line with intellectual and scientific rigor, the harder our futures will be as academics. I believe a balance is necessary.
- I think that academia tends to lean left; I know that in thirty-plus years as a member of five university faculties, I have heard a great deal of disdain expressed for opinions not in conformity with the prevailing ones. That certainly discourages research that might lead to unpopular conclusions (e.g., unflattering studies of green energy sources, work that does not support anthropogenic climate change, and the like). For all the talk about the value of diversity, unorthodox political opinions—at least those that lean right—do not appear to be welcome in the academic community, so any research that might support unpopular political positions is probably also discouraged. A major university like the University of Michigan could do a lot for public discourse by actively seeking out and encouraging the expression of diverse opinions from members of its community.
- Unless the research has near-term impact, there is a tendency to "hype" research to try to magnify its impact before it has really accomplished anything. I think academics should

affect public policy and the public should be informed of research, but without the tendency to spin or hype the near-term benefits.
- The above is more than enough.
- Most of these questions are very remote from my work as an engineering mathematician. I do hope you are not going to weigh everyone equally.
- On many occasions, those of us focusing on academic research tend to be isolated and/or uninformed of the needs of the general public. We do not tend to represent the "general" public. Public policy needs to serve everyone.

4. When you are engaging in or contemplating the activities listed above, what additional support do you think that U-M could/should provide?

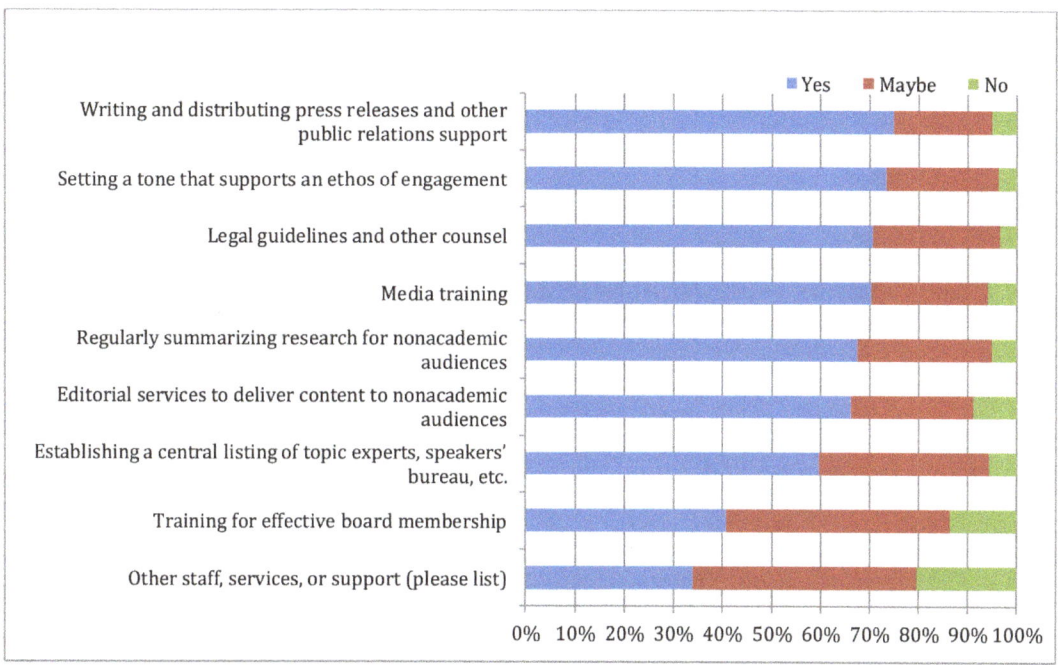

Of the respondents, 75 percent believe that U-M should be writing and distributing press releases, and 72 percent believe that U-M should set a tone that supports engagement.

Additional suggested support includes the following:

- Help faculty understand appropriate public engagement, which is no simple matter.
- Provide infrastructure support for staff for different entities on campus to engage in this type of work: staff services, website/blogging support, library support.
- Lower the administrative load overall.
- Provide grant application assistance for engaged projects.
- Create university-wide publications that demonstrate public engagement and relevance.
- Train tenure and promotion committees on what should qualify as success in regards to community-engaged scholarship.
- Provide legal protection.

- Hire PR staff to help write summaries for nonacademic audiences and media people with an understanding of what we do.
- Translate work for non-English-speaking communities.
- Actively make community engagement part of tenure.
- Offer funding or travel assistance for congressional or other high-value public testimony; finance entrepreneurial efforts by faculty.
- I feel U-M does many of these things. I would be concerned with one-size-fits-all board membership.

www.ingramcontent.com/pod-product-compliance
Lightning Source LLC
Chambersburg PA
CBHW060949170426
43201CB00027B/2428

www.ingramcontent.com/pod-product-compliance
Lightning Source LLC
Chambersburg PA
CBHW060949170426
43201CB00027B/2428